BEGINNER'S GUIDE TO CURLING

D1556875

BEGINNER'S GUIDE TO
CURLING

ROBIN WELSH

PELHAM BOOKS

First published in Great Britain by
PELHAM BOOKS LTD
52 Bedford Square
*London, W.C.*1
OCTOBER 1969
SECOND IMPRESSION MARCH 1970
© 1969 *by Robin Welsh*

7207 0303 4

Set and printed in Great Britain by
Tonbridge Printers Ltd, Peach Hall Works, Tonbridge, Kent
in Baskerville eleven on thirteen point on paper supplied by
P. F. Bingham, and bound by James Burn
at Esher, Surrey

CONTENTS

ILLUSTRATIONS

ACKNOWLEDGEMENTS

The author's grateful thanks are due to the following,
whose photographs illustrate this book:
The Scotsman: Photos. Nos. 2, 3; *Alex C. Cowper,
Perth*: 6, 53; *Francis C. Inglis, Edinburgh*: 7; *Photograph by Gerry Cranham,* courtesy *The Observer*: 8;
Murray Donald, Edinburgh: 9, 10, 11, 12, 13, 18–29,
30–41, 42–45, 46; *Photo Illustrations, Edinburgh*: 14,
15; *Michael Burns, Toronto*: 16, 48, 49, 52; *D.
Whyte's Studio, Inverness*: 17; *Erwin F. Nell, Wis-
consin*: 50; *Lars-Olof Magnil, Stockholm*: 51.

CHAPTER ONE

THE HISTORY OF THE GAME

CURLING IS CALLED the 'roarin' game', not because of the shouts of carefree curlers but because of the roar a curling stone makes as it travels, particularly on outside ice. Two hundred years ago, a young Scot, James Graeme (1749–1772), a native of Carnwath in Lanarkshire, composed a poem, excerpts from which are still used on menus at curling suppers. Graeme provided the best onomatopoeic description of the 'roar' when he wrote of a stone gliding along, *hoarse murmuring.*

The noise of stones is heard to the best advantage on a hillside overlooking a bonspiel on a frozen Scottish loch. In the stillness of a clear frosty morning, the distinctive deep-throated boom reverberates through the valley and into the hills. The sound, like the ocean's roar, is the music of Curling.

> '. . . the sweetest sound tae me
> Is music o' the channel-stane
> Gaun currin' tae the tee.'*

How far does the sound reach back in time? No one knows. The origin of curling is lost in the mists which also shroud the origin of golf, the other great game which Scotland has given to the world.

The first landmark used in curling histories is the Stirling Stone, which has the date 1511 etched on one side. This famous old stone, which lies in the Smith Institute, Stirling, is a 26-pound Kuting (or quoiting or coiting) stone, the earliest-known form of stone used for curling, which, in its infancy, must have been a form of quoiting on ice.

* H. Shanks, Bathgate, 1884.

Stirling has an honoured place in Scottish and curling history. The Stirling Stone lies in the shade of the Wallace Monument, the towering memorial to the Scottish patriot. Nearby, the old Borestone Club, now the Borestone and Stirling Club, made a curling pond on the site of the Milton Bog where the Scots routed the English cavalry at Bannockburn in 1314. (The Borestone Club took its name from the 'Borestone', on which King Robert the Bruce placed his standard at the battle.)

On one side of the Stirling Stone is the inscription 'St. Js. B. STIRLING 1511' – a reference, according to Captain Macnair in *The Channel Stane* (1883) either to St James, a popular saint in Stirling, 'B' possibly being a contraction for 'Bridge', or the St James Hospital which was known to have stood at the Bridge-end of Stirling before the Reformation. On the other side of the stone are the words, 'A GIFT'.

It is fair to state that experts believe these inscriptions to be of a later date, perhaps a much later date, than 1511. There is doubt, as in so many matters concerned with the early history of the game, but, without doubt, the Stirling Stone, made of the same blue whinstone as Stirling Rock, is very old.

Even older in appearance are the two other stones which lie alongside it in the Institute. Both are more irregular, more primitive – one, of rough triangular shape, weighing $15\frac{3}{4}$ pounds. The other, a longer stone broken at one end, weighs $20\frac{1}{2}$ pounds; a channel whinstone, its sides have been pared down by a mason to reduce its weight. It was found by Mr James Sword, Curator of the Smith Institute, in 1890, in a dyke at a blacksmith's door in the hamlet of Chartershall – near the Whins of Milton village on the site of the Milton Bog. Almost certainly, the stone was reclaimed from the bog, which, having served Scotland so well at Bannockburn, was drained in 1840.

The present Curator of the Museum, Mr James Thomson, reports that the stones attract curlers from many parts of the world and that they gaze earnestly through the glass case at the end of their pilgrimage.

Kuting stones are also known as 'channel stanes' – so called because they were taken from the channels of rivers and were thus worn smooth; and 'loofies', loof being the old Scots word for the palm of the hand – the earliest stones were shaped like a palm and had grooves for fingers and thumb. Such stones were thrown through the air to the ice with a sideways action, like the reverse sweep of a scythe.

The controversy, whether curling started in Scotland or the Low Countries, still rages. Two landscapes by the great Flemish painter, Pieter Breughel (1530–1569) add fuel to fiery discussions. These works, *Hunters in the Snow* and *The Bird Trap,* show a game resembling curling being played on frozen ponds.

The controversy should not be taken too seriously. The man mainly responsible for it was the Rev. John Ramsay* (1777–1871) whose book, *An Account of the Game of Curling by a Member of the Duddingston Curling Society* (Edinburgh 1811) is the oldest historical record of the game.

Ramsay wrote: 'We have all the evidence which etymology can give in favour of curling's Continental origin. The terms, being all Dutch or German, point to the Low Countries as the place in which it most probably originated, or, at least, from whence it was conveyed to us. For if it was not introduced from the Continent, but was first invented in this country, it must have been at a time when the German and Low Dutch were the prevailing languages. Now, though the Saxon was once pretty general in this country, and there are still many Dutch words in our language, yet those German dialects were never so general as to make it credible that our countrymen, in any particular invention, would employ them alone as the appropriate terms. In the history of inventions such a phenomenon is not to be found. Had there been only one or two foreign terms, these would not have militated much against the domestic origin of the

---

* Ramsay, born at Carstairs, graduated at Edinburgh University, and edited *The Scots Magazine* for two years while studying Theology. He was Minister at Ormiston for 20 years and, for the last 38 years of his life, at Gladsmuir, and it was said of him: 'of nothing was he prouder than of the share he had taken in introducing and popularising the game of Curling in the County of Haddington'.

game but the whole of the terms being Continental compel us to ascribe to it a Continental origin.'

This dictatorial statement, which was blindly accepted and repeated by later historians, was challenged by the Rev. John Kerr, whose *History of Curling* (Edinburgh 1890) remains the classic book on the history and growth of the game. Refuting Ramsay's theories, Kerr enlisted eminent professors of his day to clear the air and one of these, Professor Masson,* a famous personality of the time, took a firm stand against Ramsay's views :

'I see no proof in them (the terms) collectively that the game came from the Continent. Most of the terms are of Teutonic origin in a general way; some are of French origin; some might even be claimed as of Celtic original; and a few seem recent inventions by the natural *nous* of players of the game within the last century or so, to define recurring circumstances and incidents of the game previously unnamed. I do not think much can be made for your question on either side by chasing up etymologies. The matter seems mainly a historical one.

'Wherever there was ice, there must have been, since man existed, games on the ice; and the question is whether the particular game of Curling can be proved to have been in use anywhere out of Scotland without clear derivation from Scotland. If it ever existed anywhere else, it ought to be found in that place now; for, the ice still remaining, the extinction of the game, if once in use, may be voted impossible. Curlers, therefore, ought to drive at this question : Is there any Curling now, or anything like Curling, anywhere in the world out of Scotland, except by obvious and probable derivation from Scotland?

'The terms of the game, on the supposition of its Scottish origin, are easily accounted for. The original inventors of the game, or of the germ of the present game, would use the words

* David Masson, Professor of English Literature at Edinburgh University, was the author of the well-known book, *Edinburgh Sketches and Memories.*

Left: John Cairnie, the one-armed surgeon whose personality and drive inspired the formation of the Grand Caledonian Curling Club in 1838, the title being changed, because of Royal patronage, to the Royal Caledonian Curling Club in 1843. John Cairnie who built Curlinghall, Largs, for his retirement, was the first President of the 'Grand' Club. (The original picture is owned by A. Maxtone Graham, Aberlady Mains House, Aberlady). *Below:* The Earl of Elgin (*left*), President of the Royal Club from 1967 to 1969, and Tom P. Stewart, who was elected President in July, 1969

In happy mood, The Duke of Edinburgh jokes with office bearers after his election as President of the Royal Caledonian Curling Club in 1964. Right centre is Major Allan Cameron, President in 1963–64

of their composite Scoto-English vocabulary – mostly Teutonic but some French and some Celtic for the purposes and situations of the game, just as they would for any other business; and, as the game grew, other words would be added for new developments of it or new intricacies, some of these with no antique reference in them at all.'

To these findings, the Rev. John Kerr added a letter from Amsterdam which quoted Mr H. C. Ragge, Keeper of Amsterdam University Library, as saying : 'I believe I may assume that Curling or a game similar to it has never been in use in this Country.' (It must be said that, if the two men knew of Breughel, they apparently did not know the two landscapes concerned).

Two significant points emerge from Professor Masson's findings :

1. *'Wherever there was ice, there must have been, since man existed, games on the ice.'*

In the Ice Age, or, even more appropriately in the Stone Age, a hairy monster, draped in skins, hurled the first boulder down the ice, to be followed by another monster, who tried to outhurl his opponent; and these two primitive men, eventually tiring of brute strength, set marks on the ice and the game of Curling was born.

The myth could be reality. It is as reasonable as any other conjecture on the birth of the game.

2. *'Is there any Curling now, or anything like Curling, anywhere in the world out of Scotland, except by obvious and probable derivation from Scotland?'*

To this pertinent question, we answer, firmly and confidently, 'No, there is not'.

What then, of Breughel's paintings? In the first edition of Jamieson's Scottish Dictionary (1808), it was suggested : 'Can it be supposed that this West Country name (Kuting – the earliest form of curling) has been softened from Teut. Kluyten?' Ramsay writing three years later, quickly grasped the suggestion to support his theories. Kluyten, according to Kilian's *Etymologicon Teutonical Linguae* (1632), was a Dutch game played on the ice 'with lumps or balls frozen'; and, in Dutch, the word Klyten signifies 'a clod'.*

Substantial supporting evidence for the claim that curling originated in Scotland is provided by the wide variety of old stones which, over hundreds of years, have been salvaged from lochs and ponds and unearthed in old buildings and diggings throughout the country. The Rev. John Kerr brought the full weight of his argument to bear. 'It is absurd,' he wrote, 'to suppose that, if the game were Flemish and carried with Flemings wherever they settled, it would only be in Scotland that the primitive stones would be found.'

The question, even more pertinent than Professor Masson's, is: If curling was once played in the Low Countries, or any other country, why are there no relics of stones in any country other than Scotland?

The reasonable answer is that Breughel's game on the ice was played with frozen clods of earth which disintegrated when the thaw came – as the claims for overseas origin now disintegrate before our eyes. For a game on ice without stones cannot reasonably be called curling.

The pioneers of the past are lost in darkness and likely to remain so. But, whether the first curlers were Scots, Dutch or prehistoric men, one thing is certain: Scotsmen nurtured the game, regulated it, exported it to many lands and brought it to its present peak of popularity. The curling chain, forged in Scotland, now spans the world with links in 14 countries, and, as new countries and new clubs join the chain, the bonds of curling fellowship grow ever stronger.

---

* The Game of Eisschiessen (Ice shooting), played on ice with a wooden 'stone' and long stick-like handle, is an ancient national game in Bavaria and is played elsewhere in Europe. The Icelandic 'Knattleir' was a game played with bowls on ice. Both games may be forty-second cousins of Curling; they cannot be said to have any closer relationship.

CHAPTER TWO

A SERMON ON STONES

As WE HAVE seen, kuting stones, channel stanes or loofies are the oldest curling implements known to us. The maximum weight of the examples which have survived is around 25 pounds, the smallest weighing no more than five or six pounds.

As we can suppose that these stones were thrown part of the way along the ice in a quoit-like game, it is not surprising that they were small and light, in some cases little more than large pebbles. What *is* surprising is the immense size of the boulders which appeared in the next stage of curling-stone development. The shift from one extreme to the other was caused by the insertion of a rough handle – a move so simple that curlers of the period, surveying the phenomenon, must have looked quizzically at each other and said: 'Now, why didn't I think of that?'

There is evidence that the quoiting stone and the handled stone were in use together for a period after the introduction of the handle more than 300 years ago, and, indeed, there are stones with notches for fingers and thumb with an iron handle inserted alongside.

> Gae, get twa whinstanes, round and hard,
> Syne on their taps twa thorn-roots gird,
> Then soop the ice for mony a yard,
> And mak' baith tee and colly.*

Roughly speaking, handled stones made their appearance in the first half of the 17th century. The handles – iron, wood or

* From an Old Song published in the *Scots Magazine*.

'crooked thorn' – were set in the stones by the curlers themselves or by the local blacksmith, who did a more workmanlike job.

The stones came in all shapes – conical, oval, square, three-neukit, pudding, rectangular, hexagonal and shapes which defy description – and all sizes, from large to larger.

A solid handle with which to swing a stone offered a challenge, full of exciting new possibilities, to the curling community in Scotland. The challenge was taken up in the wrong way. Instead of striving for greater skill and finesse with a controlled swing, curlers hurled their rough boulders with all their power, vying with each other in trials of strength with bigger and ever bigger stones.

Legends of mighty deeds with giant-sized blocks have been passed down in parish histories. Lochmaben curlers were proud of their President, who, at the beginning of the 19th century, accepted a challenge thrown out by Laurie Young of Tinwald. The President took his stone and threw it with such power that it sped almost a mile across the Mill Loch and hit the bank at the far side, tumbling on the grass. 'Now', said the President to Laurie Young, 'go and throw it back again and we'll confess that you're too many for us!'

> . . . Long swings the stone,
> Then with full force, careering furious on,
> Rattling, it strikes aside both friend and foe
> Maintains its course and takes the victor's place.*

We hear that, on the ice at Denny, William Gourlay's 72-pound stone struck a guard 'full' and then moved on, hitting half-a-dozen other stones before gaining the shot which was thought to be impossible. It is some of the old tales which are 'impossible', or, at least, they have gained in the telling over the 'Beef and Greens' at curlers' suppers! This middle era of curling was the blood-and-thunder period of the game when strong-arm methods were needed to reach the

* From *British Georgics* by James Grahame.

tee which was hidden by a wall of formidable stones and when the hero was carried shoulder-high from the bonspiel for blasting his way to victory.

> An' many a broken channel-stane
> Lay scattered up an' down

wrote David Davidson, a Kirkcudbright poet, of a stirring battle in 1789.

What a waste of stones, you might say. Not so. In these days, stones cost nothing, except the effort to lift them from rivers or dykes.

Another of the objects of a really big stone must have been to manoeuvre it into the house, from which position it would not be easily dislodged. It was said of the huge Lochmaben 'Hen'; 'When once she settled, there she clockit!' How frustrating it must have been to play a perfect strike and watch your stone – possibly in several pieces – bounce off the winner without moving it!

A further frustration in these olden days was caused by the system of play, eight men forming a side and playing one stone each – in games which lasted until one side scored 21, 31 or even 51 shots. When a modern curler misses with his first stone, he is all the more determined to atone with his second. The old-time curler did not have the consolation of a second chance.

For the very reason that each curler had only one curling stone, the misshapen boulders became objects of special veneration and were affectionately christened by their owners. The Hen, The Horse, The Cockit-hat, The Bannock, Whirlie, The Grey Mare, The Bible, Black Meg, The Whaup, Buonaparte, The Prince, Wallace, Hughie and hundreds more created a saga of stones in the parish bonspiels which for centuries fostered the rivalry and fellowship which is the stuff of curling.

> Rivalry and good fellowship,
> The twin pillars of the Bonspiel.
> Old Toast.

The majority of these handled stones weighed between 35 and 75 pounds but there were some massive blocks which could only have been wielded by men of unusual strength. The Egg (115 pounds), belonging to the Blairgowrie and Delvine Clubs, The Saut Backet (116 pounds) from Couper Angus and the supreme example of strength for strength's sake, The Jubilee Stone* (117 pounds) are monuments to the giants of the past.

The way our ancestors threw these cumbersome masses is a source of wonder, especially to those who find it difficult enough to throw a modern stone into the rings on drug (dour) ice.

Old stones are preserved in many of the Local Clubs in Scotland, often being displayed at curling suppers or used at Curlers' Courts. Many have served as weights on hay ricks and to keep thatch on roofs. Others have become door stops. Some have been relegated to lowly positions as foot-scrapers at front doors and some have been incorporated in battlements and other buildings, like the small loofie found embedded in a wall in Edinburgh's Royal Mile.

The relics, found in all parts of Scotland, constitute a massively eloquent 'sermon on stones', which is part of the nation's heritage.

But, however nostalgic we may feel about those older days, we are glad they have passed. Graded stones have raised the game to a fine art. Brain is now the victor over brawn.

The history of curling is the history of curling stones and a search among stones yields evidence of changes much more

---

* The Jubilee Stone, presented to the Royal Caledonian Curling Club by John Wilson, Chapelhill, Cockburnspath, was exhibited at the Jubilee Meeting of the Royal Club in 1888. It belonged to John Hood, who died at Townhead in 1888. He had seen his father curl with the stone and had used it himself. The Stone is now displayed with other Royal Club relics in Perth Ice Rink and it is interesting to know that Thomas Hood, a descendant of John Hood, still farms Townhead and is a keen curler. He believes that the Jubilee Stone was taken from the sea at the Mouth of the Pease Burn at Cockburnspath and was then laid upside down at the entrance to stables for a season so that the running surface could be worn smooth by horses' hooves.

revolutionary in their nature than historical changes in golf tennis, rugby, cricket or, indeed, any game of which we can think.

The transformation from quoiting on ice to curling is bewildering enough. But the far more radical change from the rough boulder to the rounded stone is easily the most important revolution in the history of curling.

Towards the end of the 18th century, some genius, or, more likely, an average curler with a degree of perception, noticed that stones more spherical than others gave a higher standard of performance. Perhaps, also, as in many inventions, the discovery was made in different places at the same time and slowly evolved in several areas – eventually to take the curling community by storm.

The rounding of the stone changed the whole aspect of play and brought uniformity and order to the game. The new stone not only ran consistently but rebounded consistently from other stones, making angled raises or wicks as predictably possible as billiard shots.

A premium on accuracy was immediately established and the game became a test of skill, not strength. In addition, a curler could now control the curved line taken by a round stone. By turning the handle of a stone, thus applying 'in-hand' or 'out-hand' motion – like the bias in bowls – stones 'curled' in paths which could be predetermined.

As in the case of the handle, the rounding of the stone seemed a natural and obvious evolution. But how long it took curlers to grasp the obvious! Is it possible that another remarkable, and remarkably simple, advance in the evolution of our game will soon be made, and that, at any moment, some average curler, or group of curlers, will see the 'natural' and 'obvious' and spring the discovery on a startled world?

During the 19th century, circular stones from established areas were the vogue. The best-known types included Ailsas – quarried from the famous little island of Ailsa Craig in the Clyde which, for more than 100 years, has given stones to the curlers of the world – Burnock Waters, Crawfordjohns,

Blantyres, Tinkernhills, Carsphairns and Crieffs, so called because of the localities which supplied the stone. All had different
properties. Curlers chose those they thought best suited to the
conditions on their local lochs or ponds.

In curling literature through the years, curling stones have
been called 'granites', but, under recent reclassification by
geologists, this is not now strictly true. The important thing
about the stone used for modern curling is that it must have a
consistent hardness and toughness, as any soft minerals among
the harder ones will result in uneven wear.* Careful selection is
therefore imperative. The stone also has a homogeneous quality
which binds it together and prevents flaking. A fine grain provides a strong interlocking structure, and, in addition, a low
water absorbency; when stones dry out, the fine crystals are not
dislodged by the outflow of water as heavier crystals would be.
This is why curling stones are not brittle, why they seldom chip.
This is why a good pair of curling stones lasts a lifetime.†

When stones were rounded, their weight dropped to manage-
able proportions. Polishing and other refinements were added,
like striking bands to preserve the stones and concave bases with
running rims. Reversible stones, with dull and keen sides, were
introduced; these stones, cupped on one side only, are not now
manufactured. On the flat, keen side, the stone travelled further
on dull ice but it slithered along, often out of control, without
drawing or 'taking the hand'.

Today, with the advent of indoor Ice Rinks and the high
quality of ice-making in the countries not yet served by indoor
Rinks, curling stones have been standardised – or very nearly so.

In general, stones for indoor curling are now made with cups
5 inches in diameter on top and bottom. For outdoor play in

* Many countries outside Scotland have tried to manufacture curling
stones. Up to now, they have not found a stone with the properties
required for this specialised job.

†In busy Ice Rinks, where matched sets of stones are used daily from
morning to night, it is estimated that stones will last for perhaps ten
years – five years' running on each side. Then they can be re-ground,
to sharpen the running edges, with a loss of approximately half-a-pound
in weight each time the operation is carried out.

The most famous of all curling paintings – *The Curlers*, by Sir George Harvey, P.R.S.A. Two similar works were painted by the artist. One is owned by Gilbert McClung, Edinburgh; the other hangs in the National Gallery of Scotland in Edinburgh

Above: The first Grand Match of the Royal Club at Penicuik House, High Pond, on January 15, 1847. (The original oil painting is owned by Sir John Clerk, Bart.. Penicuik House, Penicuik.) *Below:* Willie Murray (*right*), Convener of the Grand Match Committee of the Royal Club, on Loch Leven with Tom Stark (*second right*) and other helpers. Tom Stark, who for many years has supervised the laying-out and marking of the 300 rinks required for a Grand Match between North and South of Scotland, holds a tee-ringer for cutting circles on the ice. Willie Murray holds an axe for breaking the ice and a stick for measuring the thickness of ice. Snow scrapers are also shown

Switzerland, where big variations are caused by sunshine and shade, stones with 3½-inch and 4½-inch cups are used, and, in Sweden, the outside stones are cupped 4 inches on one side and 5 inches on the other.

The general rule is: cups of smaller diameter with a dulled running edge for outdoor play; and 5-inch cups with a finer running edge for indoor play.

After learning the game in the big Ice Rinks, newcomers to curling in Scotland will be keen to participate in outdoor bonspiels and to share the exhilaration and companionship of a day spent under a wintry sky in cauld, cauld, frosty weather. Many Scottish Clubs own their own outdoor stones, for use when the frost comes. If more pairs are needed – for large-scale bonspiels like the Grand Match of the Royal Caledonian Curling club,* for example – well-used indoor stones with dulled running edges are suitable on normal ice.

A modern curling stone is a thing of beauty, its smooth and polished surface made more beautiful by reflected shades of blue, red or grey. It is a pity that many Ice Rinks cover the tops of their matched sets of stones with coloured plastic caps. The object – to make the stones of the opposing sides more easily identifiable – is achieved but much of the intrinsic beauty of the stone and the skill of the stone-makers' art is lost to view.

Many Ice Rinks have also introduced plastic handles. Unattractive to look at, they adversely change the 'feel' of the grip and in many cases cause an unusual hollow thud when two stones meet – as if the stones were complaining about their 'handling'!

The provision of matched sets of stones in the Scottish Ice Rinks is a recent development which began only 10 years ago. Before that, each curler had his own pair of stones and Ice Rinks were lined with serried rows of lockers, in which thousands of stones were housed. Great was the activity each day as the appropriate stones were lifted from lockers to the ice, to be returned after each session and replaced by other groups – and great was the wrath of the curler whose favourite stones had, for

* Hereafter called the 'Royal Club'.

a variety of reasons, been forgotten. (It was no use putting the stones on the ice at the start of the game as stones require a three-hour period to cool before play).

This was hard labour for Ice Rink staffs who heaved a huge sigh of relief when matched sets were introduced. These sets remain on the ice for all sessions and are used by all curlers who are not now permitted to play their own stones.

Under the Rules of Curling, formulated by the Royal Club, 'all curling stones shall be of a circular shape. No stone, including handle and bolt, shall be of greater weight than 44 pounds or of greater circumference than 36 inches, or of less height than one-eighth part of its greatest circumference'. The stones in general use in the Scottish Ice Rinks weigh 40 pounds each. The addition of one and a half pounds for the handle and bolt make the total weight to be thrown 41½ pounds.

Many people who do not curl know that the average weight of a curling stone is 40 pounds but few curlers know how a stone is made. Very simply, the stages are :

1. The rock is blasted. The pieces are carefully examined and only stone of good texture is selected. This is rough-hewn into fat, round blocks weighing roughly 100 pounds.

2. The blocks are then matched in colour and texture into pairs and sets of four pairs.

3. Having been matched, each stone is roughed down to a size 12 pounds heavier than its finished weight. Then a hole is bored exactly through the centre.

4. The stone is then turned in a lathe 'between centres' and reduced by circular cutter to within two pounds of the final weight. Then follows the grinding process and formation of the cup and the rim. The rim, the running edge of the stone, is all-important and must be precisely positioned.

5. Now within a few ounces of its final weight, the stone is placed on a vertical shaft and polished. It is at this stage that the running edge is carefully finalised to suit ice requirements.

6. The stone, now smooth and glistening, is then given its striking band, or 'belt'.

7. Finally, the holes already bored, are countersunk square to receive the iron bolts which take the handles.

And now the stones are ready to skim the ice of the world, for Scottish stones, which have qualities which cannot be matched elsewhere, are sent to every curling country overseas.

CHAPTER THREE

THE PARAPHERNALIA OF THE GAME

HANDLES :

We have seen that the first handles inserted in stones were made of iron, wood or thorn. When stones were rounded, towards the end of the eighteenth century, more sophisticated handles were introduced. Among the first of these were the 'Dalmellington hands', from Dalmellington in Ayrshire, which were set in holes cut between the centre and side of stones.

Handles became increasingly beautiful and ornate. The nineteenth century examples were made of brass, gun metal, bone; they were nickel-plated or made of solid nickel or even solid silver. The handles were richly mounted in ebony, buffalo horn, vulcanite and ivory. They were items to be prized, and, indeed, were given as prizes or awarded to curlers for services to the game or the local club.

When ice began to still the waters on Scottish lochs, curlers would polish the handles of their stones . . .

> auld handles, wi' an age untold,
> are made to shine like minted gold.*

When the manufacture of stones became centralised in a few factories, and matched sets were produced, handles were standardised. Today, they are made of brass or bronze, chromium-plated; and, in some cases, which we hope will diminish but fear will not, of plastic.

HACKS AND CRAMPITS :

The equipment needed for curling is simple in design and

* James Hogg (the Ettrick Shepherd).

24

straightforward in use, Consider the 'Hack', the implement from which a curling stone is thrown.

In its simplest form, the hack is, as its name implies, not an implement at all but a hole in the ice. It began as a hole, and, after many vicissitudes through the ages, it is a hole again in many parts of the world.*

At outdoor bonspiels in Scotland today, the ice is still hacked by some curlers and the foot inserted in the hole as a purchase for throwing curling stones. It is the oldest 'foothold' in the game. The curlers of Sanquhar, for many years a principal stronghold of the game, cut a notch in the ice, in which a curler placed the side of the foot, and this practice was followed in Lanarkshire and elsewhere.

It is also the most modern. In Canada and the United States, where curling is almost exclusively an indoor sport, the sunken hack, as it is called, is universal. The hole is lined with rubber to give stability and to prevent slipping.

This form of hack, which provides the most secure base for delivery, is not used in the Scottish Ice Rinks for one simple reason : on a sheet of ice which is also used for skating it is not practical to fill the hack-holes before skating and to cut new holes before the next curling session. In these circumstances, a raised hack, with prongs which fit into small holes bored in the ice, is used. It is lifted before the skaters take the ice, and – a most important and too often neglected point – should also be lifted after each end of play in case a player, with his mind on other things, trips over it behind the rings at the next end. In Scotland, a standard rubber-covered hack, proposed by the Royal Club, is in general use in the Ice Rinks.

Many curlers believe that the crampit as we know it in Scotland is the oldest type of grip for delivering stones. This popular misconception is very wide of the mark. The crampit is, in fact, the modern form of the foot-iron introduced early in the 19th

---

* The Rev. John Kerr, in his *History of Curling* 1890, stated that the hole in the ice was not the oldest form of foothold but a later development. It is one of the few findings in Kerr's great book with which we disagree.

century by John Cairnie, first President of the Royal Club, the one-armed, single-minded naval surgeon whose name shines brightly in the annals of curling. Cairnie's foot-iron was a piece of sheet-iron three feet nine inches long by nine inches wide, punched or well frosted on both sides and turned up about an inch at the end to give purchase to the back foot.

By coincidence, however, the earliest contrivances used as holds for hurling curling stones were also called crampits (or cramps or tramps). But they were very different instruments, being iron or steel pads, with prongs underneath, which were attached to the feet by straps.

They were in use in Scotland until the middle of the nineteenth century and there was considerable controversy before Cairnie's foot-irons were generally adopted in place of the strapped-on crampits or tramps. Cairnie called these crampits 'almost barbarous' but, in 1830, Sir Richard Broun, in his *Memorabilia Curliana Mabenensia,* stated forcibly: 'It must ever be kept in view, however, that sweeping forms a most important item in the Curler's task. Nor can we see how this can properly be performed unless the player stands *sicker* upon the ice. The alert sweeper has little in common with the mincing steps of the slip-shod looker-on. He who cannot play a scientific game in tramps, will never play one out of them.'* So that curlers did not merely throw their stones with tramps attached to their boots but also ran all over the ice on them; this is one Rule which has changed with a vengeance, the pertinent regulation today being 'no player shall wear boots, tramps, or sandals with spikes, or other contrivance which may break or damage the surface of the ice'.

The main trouble with these strapped-on grips was that, if an opposing stone was guarded, it was simplicity itself to take a step or two to the right or left to make the shot easier – an

---

* Condemning the practice, a Kilmarnock curler wrote, in 1830: 'We cannot conceive how a crampetted player can attend to the sweeping of stones without so mangling the ice as to make it unfit for use. Shoes, and a kind of boots, made of carpet, dreadnought, or felt, are in universal use. With felt shoes, a man may walk or run on the keenest ice.'

advantage to the player but a disadvantage to the game. The first Rules of the Royal Club, published in 1839, came down hard on the practice in these words in Rule 6 : 'A player stepping aside to take a brittle (or wick), or other shot, shall forfeit his stone for that end.'

Other old grips used in varying forms by the Clubs of Scotland were the trickers (triggers, grippers or crisps). The remarkable feature of these is that they were made in sets, one to hold the heel of the right foot, the other for the toe of the left foot. The game of curling must have been a 'tricky' business in those days !

The modern form of crampit is still used in Scotland but the preference for it is fading fast. Curlers who were *thirled* on it continue to use it but the new curlers who are flocking to the game in their thousands invariably start on the hack and it is reasonable to anticipate that, apart from outdoor bonspiels, the crampit will soon disappear from the Scottish scene.

When the indoor Ice Rinks were established in Glasgow and Edinburgh in 1907 and 1912, the crampit was the vogue and curlers gazed in awe when Col. T. S. G. H. Robertson Aikman, President of the Royal Club in 1924–25, brought his own type of hack to the ice. His invention, made of wood, was a much bigger version of the hack now used (see Plate 13 facing page 65) but we believe that the Colonel, whose son, Bill Robertson Aikman, followed him as Royal Club President (1965 to 1967), was a prime mover in popularising the hack in modern Scottish curling. When the Colonel introduced his hack, which, as Captain of the Royal Club team, he took to Canada in 1912, several curlers from the West of Scotland used 'crisps' (metal hacks) in the Scottish Ice Rink in Glasgow.

THE DUSTER :

Suffering an even steeper decline than the crampit is the duster which was used by almost all Scottish skips until a few years ago. The duster, often a yellow car cloth, sometimes a handkerchief or a bundle of coloured wool, was employed as a marker, indicating the place where the stone should come to rest, or, when placed on top of a stone, the stone to be hit. The cry 'You're right on the duster' rang through the Ice Rinks but is now scarcely heard, the duster being virtually obsolete.

THE BOTTLE AND THE DOLLY :

Equipment now extinct in Scotland includes the tee-marker (a misshapen wooden skittle) which showed the position of the tee or centre of the circles. This all-important spot, which is the aim of all curlers, was originally indicated by a button, a bawbee (a half-penny) or a pinch of snuff. Later, a special iron ring with a prong was pressed down on the ice. Later still, a wooden bottle* marked the spot; still used in Points Competitions (see Rules Section), it is never seen in normal games.

But its big sister, the Dolly, a squatter and fatter 'bottle', plays a major role on the ice in many parts of Europe as a tee-marker, and has been honoured by Geneva curlers, whose 'Dolly Cup' is one of the most important Swiss competitions.

The Dolly tends to obstruct stones, or even become checked between stones if the skip is not alert enough to lift it out of harm's way, and the Rule concerning the Dolly places the onus of blame firmly on the skip using it at the time.

TASSELS, BASKETS :

Tassels – little baubles of coloured wool attached to the handles of stones – have been superseded in Scotland by coloured plastic discs which cover the tops of stones for identification, each side playing with eight stones of one colour. But tassels are used everywhere in Switzerland and other parts of the Continent and Scandinavia, and stones are transported there, as they once were in Scotland, in handsome baskets, now almost unknown here.

BESOMS, BROOMS AND BRUSHES :

A cutting from the osier tree was the earliest curling besom we know of. The twigs of the osier, a species of willow, are used for

---

* 'The Delvine Bottle', used by the Delvine Club in Perthshire (instituted 1732), was a wooden replica of a quart whisky bottle complete with cork. 'Come to the bottle', 'guard the bottle' and 'smell the bottle' were well-known expressions on outdoor ice.

basket-making, and cricket bats have been traditionally made from willow. Our curling ancestors found its slender, pliant branches ideal for sweeping snow from the ice and for encouraging laggard stones.

Brooms were made of twigs of broom bound together and old-time curlers did not call them besoms but kowes or cowes. Birch, blaeberry and other varieties of trees and plants were used for broom-making through the ages and kowes came to be recognised as the twigs of any plant or shrub tied together.

When the Royal Club rules were first published, in 1839, Rule 15 began: 'Every player to come provided with a besom.' From the earliest times, when a curler cut his besom from a tree, to the beautifully-fashioned, brightly-painted brooms of today, the value of a good broom has been recognised by curlers. Sweeping has always played a major part in the game. (See the Chapter on Sweeping).

Last century, delicately-made brooms, with small tightly-bound sweeping areas and curved walking-stick handles, were much sought after. Silver bands were wrapped round the handles for inscriptions and the brooms were played for in Club competitions in Scotland – the trophies being comparable to old-style Putters, suitably engraved, which are competed for at golf.

Two main types of besom are used today – the brush in Scotland and Europe generally and the corn broom or whisk broom in Canada and the United States. The use of the two types is sharply divided by the Atlantic Ocean although the broom, once common on frozen lochs and ponds, is still seen on outdoor ice in Scotland; and, following tours by Scots, the brush is making its appearance in some Canadian and American Clubs.

The Corn Broom, traditionally the sweeping instrument in Canada, tends to strew straws on the ice and some clubs are experimenting with a new type of broom, made of nylon, which eliminates dirt on the ice, and, it is claimed, is cheaper and lasts longer.

Probably the best type of Scottish brush is made of horsehair. Other types are Mexican fibre, a mixture of Mexican fibre and flagged polypropylene, and pure flagged polypropylene. 'Flagged' means that the tips of the fibre have been broken up to give a softer effect. And 'polypropylene'? We are ninety-nine per cent certain that curlers have no idea that the tough man-made fibre with which they beat the ice is also used for making artificial heart valves. The game has come a long way since a curler selected a branch from a tree on his way to the bonspiel!

CHAPTER FOUR

TERMINOLOGY

THE TERMS USED in curling vary from country to country, from district to district and from curler to curler. Many of the old terms are disappearing, although some skips still use words from a previous age, and the vocabulary is much shorter and simpler now than then, if less colourful and expressive.

We will give two lists of terms, one old-time, containing expressions still heard on occasions on the Scottish ice, and the other modern.

OLD TERMS :

Be cannie!

Besom: A broom.

Birl: The turning of the handle of a stone.

Borrow: The amount of draw to left or right taken by a stone.

Chuckle: A series of inwicks.

Cowe (or Kowe): A broom.

Crack an Egg: To just touch another stone with your stone.

Drug Ice: Dour or slow ice.

Ewe Lamb: Your one stone counting among a number of opposing stones.

Fled the Tee: Past the tee.

Forehan': The lead player.

Gie it heels: Sweep the stone.

Gleg Ice: Good, keen ice.

Hin' han': The player throwing the last stones.

Howe: The middle of the ice from tee to tee.

Kep: A rest against a stone, to save your stone from going through the house.

Ne'er a Cowe: Don't sweep.

O! for a Guard!

Redd the Ice: Clear the ice before outdoor play or break up the guards to open the way to the tee or the winner.

Side Stane (or a guid side stane): A stone at a side of the house.

Soutering: To win without allowing the other side to score.

Tak' it by the Handle: Take a stone which has hogged off the ice.

Thunnerin' Cast: A stone thrown with all your strength.

Twist: The in-hand or the out-hand.

MODERN TERMS :

Back-ring Weight: The weight required to take a stone to the back ring.

Bite: A stone just touching the outside circle is said to be biting.

Bonspiel: We believe the term comes from the Belgian *bonne* (a district or village) and *spel* (play), meaning a contest within the village or between villages or parishes.

Burn: To burn a stone (see page 95).

Check: To check a stone is to lay one alongside it, normally at an angle.

Close Guard (or Short Guard): To guard alongside the shot to be guarded.

Counter: Any stone which is within the circles.

Crampit: The iron foot board from which a stone is delivered.

Dead Guard: A stone directly in front of the shot.

Double Take-out: A strike which removes two opposing stones.

Draw: A slow stone with just enough weight to reach the house (q.v.). Also the lateral movement of a stone on the ice caused by the turning of the handle.

End: An end is completed when all sixteen stones have been played.

Every Inch!: An exhortation from the skip to his sweepers to sweep hard all the way.

Fill the Port: Place a stone between two other stones so that the opposing side cannot play a stone between them.

Freeze: The same as 'Crack an Egg'.

Grand Match on Linlithgow Loch (1848) by Charles Lees, R.S.A. This painting, which contains the faces of many well-known curlers of the period, is owned by the Royal Club and hangs in Perth Ice Rink

This striking picture shows approximately half of the curlers engaged in the last Grand Match – held on the Lake of Menteith in 1963

Full Draw: A stone with enough weight at least to reach the tee.

Guard: To place a stone in front of the shot so that the opposing side cannot hit the shot directly.

Hack: Originally a notch in the ice, now a metal or rubber-covered appliance from which a stone is delivered.(The Hack is sunk in the ice in Canada and U.S.A.)

Hack-weight: The weight required to take a stone to the hack behind the circles.

Hand (Handle): The in-turn or the out-turn.

Hard!: An exhortation from the skip to sweep hard.

Head: The same as 'End' (perhaps a corruption of 'Heat'.)

Heavy: Heavy ice is dull ice. A heavy stone is one played too fast.

Hog: A stone which does not clear the hog score (q.v.) and which is removed from the ice. (May have originated from 'hog', a one-year-old sheep which tends to lag behind the flock.)

Hog Score (Hog line): The line across the ice one sixth part of the distance from the foot score to the further Tee (q.v.).

Hold: When a skip shouts 'hold', he means 'stop sweeping'.

House: The circles.

Keen Ice: Fast ice.

Kiggle-caggle: The rocking movement of a stone which is not properly soled.

Lead: The first player in a rink.

Peels: To be equal in shots, from *Peel,* a Lothian and West of Scotland word meaning to equal or to match. *Peyl-en* (Teut.) is to measure.

Port: The space between two stones.

Pot-lid (Pat-lid): A stone lying on the tee.

Promote: To strike another stone forward.

Raise: The same as 'Promote'.

Read the Ice: Study the ice and learn its features.

Rink: A sheet of ice for curling or a team of four curlers.

Roll: A stone rolls to a side after striking another stone – or 'wicks and rolls'.

Rub: A light wick on another stone. Lucky rub – a fluke.

B

Running Stone (Runner): A fast stone.

Runs (Falls): Stones take abnormal paths (runs) because of ridges or hollows on the ice.

Skip: The captain of a rink (once called director or douper). The word may have come from the Skipper of a ship.

Sole: To deliver the sole of a stone squarely on the ice.

Spiel: Shortened version of bonspiel. Once used in Scotland but not now. Common in Canada and U.S.A.

Stack Brooms: Curlers stack brooms prior to enjoying a refreshment. Often done in the middle of a social game but not recommended!

Stone (called Rock in Canada and U.S.A.)

Strike: A fast shot.

Sweep (Soop): To sweep with brooms and brushes.

Swing: An abnormally big draw.

Take the End: A skip may decide to take the end without playing his last stone because of a dangerous position.

Take-out: To remove an opposing stone.

Tee: The middle of the circles (called the Button in Canada and U.S.A.)

Tee-high: A stone which reaches the Tee-Score.

Thin (or Tight): A stone which is narrow (thrown inside the broom). Americans talk of 'pinching the broom'.

Tight Guard: The same as 'Close Guard'.

Toucher: A stone which is just touching the outside circle.

Turn: The in-turn or out-turn imparted to the handle of a stone.

Up!: Used by a skip to tell his sweepers to stop sweeping (or 'Haud up'!)

Well-laid: A stone delivered on the broom.

Wick: A stone which hits another stone on one side and rebounds at an angle.

Wide: A stone delivered outside the broom.

Winner: The shot nearest the tee.

(Note: for descriptions of other shots and terms, study the diagram of the Rink and the Rules for Points Play in Chapter 16.)

The main signals used by skips are illustrated in the photographic section.

Skips have never been a silent race and their shouts and gesticulations add to the fun and fellowship of the ice. Laurence Jackson, famous Symington curler, tells a story of one exceptional rink which played against John Robertson of Glasgow, who christened his opponents, the 'Silent Four'. None of them spoke a word and the skip made signs to indicate his requirements. John Robertson's lead, Tom MacFarlane, tried without success to coax a word out of his opposite number, who, halfway through the game, eventually came up to Tom and asked : 'Have ye electric light?'. Tom replied, 'Aye, we have', but there the conversation ended until the very last end, when the lead again approached Tom and said, slowly : 'Ye're damned lucky, we've only got candles !'

Sayings like 'Rather a hog than dae damage' and the traditional curlers' greeting, 'Keen and Clear', are well-known in the game and there are many old toasts, relics of the days when club dinners lasted for six or seven hours and almost all the members stood up to propose a Toast. Examples of these are 'Our old friend John Frost', 'Curlers' wives and sweethearts', 'The Land o' Cakes (Scotland) and her Ain Game o' Curling' and the one which every curler will drink to with special resolution, 'The Tee – what we all aim at !'

Let us add two more toasts – to Bailie Hamilton of Douglas and Deacon Jardine of Lochmaben. On a 49-yard rink, the Bailie drew through a 10-inch port three times running and the cheers of the onlookers alarmed 'The Douglas' in his castle hall. The Deacon could 'birse a needle'; having attached birses with wax to two stones, laid to form a port, and, similarly attached needles to two stones directly alongside and in line, he could draw so scientifically that, in grazing through the port, his stone would impel the birses forward through the eyes of the needles ! This must surely be the best curling 'yarn' ever spun.

To these two giants of the past, we say : 'You for a player ! Gie's a shak' o' yer hand !'

CHAPTER FIVE

OUTDOOR CURLING THROUGH THE AGES

The frost bade for abune sax ouks, till the hinner end of Feberwar.
The ice of the loch was 23, of the Brigend-Dam 18 inches thick.

IN SCOTLAND, OUTDOOR curling has been superseded to a large extent by indoor play in the big artificial Ice Rinks. But a true curler longs for frost, and, when a cold 'snap' grips the country, a sense of urgency and suspense pervades the scene.

In frosty weather, the air is expectant and this atmosphere conveys itself to curlers who pace the ground in anxious agitation, their eyes raised to the sky.

In the country districts – where, by tradition, the game has been played in the 'interlude of rural life' when the plough was frozen in the furrow – curlers inspect their local loch or pond, prepare their equipment, make sage weather forecasts – and hope. If the frost continues, meetings are hastily convened, a day is set for the bonspiel and word is quickly passed round the neighbourhood that the ice is bearing.

In the old days, it was common knowledge in the village that the tradesman or lawyer, a keen curler, would not be available for business when the temperature dropped below freezing point. Those not in the know who called would be given a cold reception.

'Is Mr Macgregor in?'
'I'm afraid not.'
'Well, when will he be back?'
'When the thaw comes!'

Such dereliction of duty, which is not unknown today, is forgivable. Consider the miserable lives led by old-time Scottish curlers. For years on end, these men, hoping and fearing, laid plans for parish bonspiels, to be thwarted by thaws. In bad years, their stones would languish in the stone house, or the attic. The frustrations caused by the vagaries of Jack Frost must have been almost too much to bear.

'Alas,' groaned a keen curler in 1883, 'the good old times seem to have passed away, when for weeks on end

> O'er burn and loch the warlock Frost
> A crystal brig would lay.*

and good ice might be confidently counted on for a long time.'

In such conditions, every advantage was taken of the opportunities for a game, and, after a spell of weary winters, curlers would often play all day and well into the night in case the dreaded thaw came the following morning.

The nineteenth century opened promisingly with a series of hard winters between 1800 and 1838. But the early 1840's were disappointing years and an *Annual* of the Royal Club of the period complained of 'the privations to which the fickle state of the thermometer has subjected us, one day raising our spirits by letting down its own to the neighbourhood of zero and the next laying prostrate all our hopes by mounting above the freezing point'.

In 1846, however, the frost returned and a song was written to celebrate the occasion:

> Johnny Frost is back again,
> The queer auld body's back again,
> Tell the news to Curling men,
> Johnny Frost is back again;

* From *The Music of the Year is Hushed,* by the Rev. Henry Duncan, Ruthwell (1774–1846), the Scot who founded the Savings Bank movement.

Johnny thocht he was to blame
For staying a' last year at hame,
Quo' he I'll just draw on my breeks
An' I'll gie them twa or three Curling weeks.

Many and various were the methods employed by curlers to gauge the conditions of frost prior to a bonspiel. A wet handkerchief, placed on the garden hedge, would be brought in at regular intervals to test its stiffness.

A ringing earth, a ringing air and a multitude of stars shining clear in a cloudless sky were favourable symptoms while bad signs were clouds in the west, a southerly wind, shooting stars, a tremulous movement of the stars and a suspicious *sough* of the wind through doorways.

James Brown, Secretary of the Sanquhar Curling Society, reported that, if a cat passed her forepaw over her ear while washing, it was a sure sign of approaching thaw. Brown also told of the dedicated curler who deliberately broke a weather glass he had recently purchased with the words : 'I'm glad to have it oot o' the hoose for there has been nae gude weather since ever I bought it !'

The winters of 1795 and 1895 shine brightly in the record books. A well-satisfied curler wrote that 'the winter of 1795 was such an one as rejoices the hearts of a' keen curlers – frosts lay lang, snaws were deep'. A Kilconquhar report of that year tells of the man who curled all day and every day for six weeks, at the end of which 'his hand actually kept the position of a person's hand holding a stone and that it kept the *crook* for a considerable time afterwards' !

Veteran curlers still with us remember that, in 1895, Loch Leven was frozen from early January until the end of March. In addition to numerous bonspiels, a wide variety of spectacular events were staged. There were skating carnivals at night to the music of pipes, melodeons and fiddles. Carriages and pairs were driven on the loch and horse-drawn sleighs were hired to drive round the historic castle in the middle of the loch where Mary Queen of Scots was imprisoned. Visitors came in special trains from all over Scotland to participate in these ice frolics, surely the gayest events of the gay nineties in Kinross-shire.

We have no record of curling during three famous winters in history – 1691, when hungry wolves entered Vienna, attacking cattle and even men; 1684, when English oaks were split by the frost and the ice on the Thames was eleven inches deep; or, the most famous of all, 1709, known as the 'cold winter', when the seas round Britain were frozen up to several miles from the shore and the frost penetrated three yards into the ground.

We know, however, that the great frost of 1746 was too much of a good thing for curlers. Church-goers on the south side of Lochwinnoch walked over the ice to the kirk on thirteen successive Sundays. Wells, fountains and burns were dried up. The ice on the loch was bent and bowed down to the bottom and curling was stopped because of the curve on the ice.

But this was an exceptional year. Complaints of too little rather than too much ice is the continuing thread in the story of Scottish curling and it is a tribute to the patient and long-suffering nature of the Scots that the game survived through so many *thin* periods.

In recent years, as in the past, outdoor curlers in Scotland have had their ups and downs, the frustrations of mild seasons being forgotten in the excitement and bonhomie of hard winters, particularly 1958–59, 1962–63 and 1967–68, when joy was unconfined for weeks on end in many parts of the country.

A hardy breed, the curling fraternity shrugs off petty ailments when the bonspiel is at hand. In the early part of the nineteenth century, the Rev. Norman Macleod captured this sturdy spirit in comic verse :

> A' nicht it was freezin', a' nicht I was sneezin',
> 'Tak care', quo' the wife, 'gudeman, o' yer cough'.
> A fig for the sneezin', hurrah for the freezin',
> For the day we're to play the bonspiel on the loch.

In addition, as the old song has it, curling is just the game for world-weary cynics, tired business men and worriers of all types :

Hae ye trouble? Hae ye sorrow?
Are ye pinched wi' warldly care?
Redd the roaring rink tomorrow,
Peuch! they'll fash ye never mair.

Scottish schools have now included curling in their curricula
(see the section on Schools' Curling). But it must be stressed that
the game can be started at any age, the term 'a young curler'
meaning a curler young in curling experience.

Some Scots threw their first stones at the age of eight or nine,
having been pressed into service when their fathers were a
man short, but the vast majority start between the ages of 20
and 50 and a fair percentage first take the ice when they retire
from business.

Those who claim they are too old to start a new sport, and
those who, feeling old, huddle round the fireside in the winter
of their lives, should be reminded of curling's powers of re-
juvenation, so aptly summed up by James Grahame in *British
Georgics* (1809):

. . . Aged men,
Smit with the eagerness of youth, are there,
While love of conquest lights their beamless eyes,
New-nerves their arms and makes them young once more.

Curling lifts the spirit and captivates the mind. The fascination
of the game itself and its aspects of teamwork and friendship are
the factors which make curling the ideal form of relaxation.

The traditions of the game have been built on the rigours and
uncertainties of outdoor play and it is obviously desirable to
continue to nurture the old outdoor connection in Scotland
while the majority of the curling population plays indoors.

There is a place for both forms in modern curling. Indeed,
after regular play in the big indoor Ice Rinks, curlers keenly
anticipate a chance to participate in outdoor bonspiels. In addition to enjoying the thrill of a day out of doors, they can take
a step into the game's history.

On occasion, outdoor ice is smooth and true – sheer perfection for curling. It can be rough, heavily biased by ridges and runs, wet, unplayable. In general, outdoor play is more chancy, less artistic, far less precise than indoor curling. But it has an invigoration all its own, the scenery, the bracing air, the bustling activity, the stops for sustenance and a drop of the 'auld kirk', the roar of stones and the fellowship under a wintry sun combining to provide an exhilaration unique in sport.

CHAPTER SIX

THE BIRTH OF THE BIRL

THE ROUNDING OF the stone brought many refinements to curling but easily the most important was the introduction of the 'in-hand' and 'out-hand' which controlled the curved path of a stone.

This rotary movement of the handle, the 'birl', was reputedly first used to advantage by Fenwick curlers and was first known as the Fenwick Twist or the Kilmarnock Twist. A song in John Cairnie's *Essay on Curling and Artificial Pond Making* (1833) contains this verse :

> Six stones within the circle stand,
> And every port is blocked,
> But Tam Pate he did turn the hand,
> And soon the port unlocked.*

The reference illustrates the most spectacular advance gained by twisting – to draw round guards – but the new method was an advantage in all types of shot. The Twist not only turned the stone but turned upside down all previous conceptions about delivering a stone. The Curler's 'Word' in the old initiation ceremony runs :

> If you'd be a curler keen,
> Look at the mark with all your een,
> Foot sure, *shoot straight* and soop clean.

* Tam Pate, a cadger from Kirk o' Shotts, played last stone in the Duke of Hamilton's rink in many famous games, particularly at Lochwinnoch in 1784. It was written: 'Tam never missed a single aim and the spectators dubbed him for a warlock.'

To shoot straight meant to deliver a stone without any 'handle' or 'birl' and to aim directly at the mark – a difficult operation since a stone which, on delivery, starts with no handle, will almost always begin to rotate one way or the other while travelling. But an in-hand or out-hand shot was considered to be a bad shot and players continued to try to shoot straight until the birth of the birl – and, in the case of many diehards, for some time after.

When twisting started to spread, at the beginning of the 19th century, it was violently opposed in conservative quarters. A curler, wryly calling himself Timothy Twist, wrote: 'There are few players who can avoid twisting their stones and this almost universal fault is the great cause of the ill success which attends their play. I have seen large parties of curlers twisting their stones and complaining with one voice of the heavy bias on the ice when the ice was perfectly level and the disappointment of the players was to be ascribed solely to the rotary motion of their stones. To guard against the habit of twisting is the first lesson to be learned by the young aspirant and he who has learned to play a straight stone has already overcome one of the greatest difficulties of the art, for, in ordinary circumstances, this is the style of play which will tell most on the success of the game.'

A Fenwick curler, John Fulton, rushed into print, in his *Account of the Scientific Movement,* to defend the revolutionary new theory:

'If I recollect aright, and I am pretty certain on that point, the first year of the century (1800) was the year of its birth. That year was memorable for the length and severity of its winter. It is told that day after day, for a period of over six weeks, a few Fenwick curlers were never absent from a small loch in this parish, on the farm of Meiklewood, then in possession of a Mr William Carse, who, being also a keen curler, was always one of the party. Here they played every imaginable shot, or 'points' as they are now termed.

'While thus engaged, they observed the effect of the rotatory motion a stone naturally takes on the ice and saw that the stone always twisted from the straight line in obedience to that motion. They felt assured that a discovery of importance to the game had been made, and that they had hit on a right principle, so they patiently set themselves to make it of practical value to curlers, and from that time to the present all young curlers in Fenwick are taught the power of twisting as an element of first-rate value, and are so taught the use of it that they know at once from the skip's broom what twist is to be used.

'We think it a scientific style of play, requiring more skill than brute force, depending much more upon intelligent calculating judgment for success than on the strong arm. With good level ice and good curlers, masters of the twist, it is very interesting and beautiful, and to a stranger, wonderful to see how the stone twists into the desired place, ignoring guards as of no consequence. But to see the twist at its best, it must be seen at Craufurdland Loch, which is perhaps the best-conditioned curling pond in Scotland, and where the ice is always the best to be found anywhere.

'There was also another circumstance which helped to make the twist a success, which was this. At the time the twist was discovered, there were living in the village of Fenwick a number of as capable young men as could be found anywhere. Intelligent and moral, active and lithe of body and limb, full of spirit for sports of all kinds, they entered with zest into the new style of curling.

'They formed themselves into four rinks, in which they played always together, and thus acquired an *esprit de corps,* a confidence in each other which made them very formidable antagonists to all comers. They were known as the Fenwick "sixteen", and, like Wellington's invincibles, could have gone anywhere.'

But many other curlers bewailed that 'the good old maxim – shoot straight' was being discarded. The controversy, which continued for many years, is remarkable to a modern curler. Indeed, the fanatical attempt to preserve a policy which maintained that the in-hand and out-hand was bad curling is probably the most fantastic single feature in a history which often soars into the realms of fantasy.

Eventually, good sense prevailed and we now play accurate shots – or it is our fault if we do not – by turning the handles of our stones.

CHAPTER SEVEN

THE ROYAL CALEDONIAN CURLING CLUB

EDINBURGH'S CONTRIBUTION TO curling has been on the grand scale. Ramsay wrote the first account of the game (1811) anonymously as 'A Member of the Duddingston Curling Society'. Curling enjoyed such a vogue in Edinburgh at the beginning of the eighteenth century that the Magistrates of the City, in ceremonial robes, paraded, in step with curling marches specially composed for the occasion, to open the season on the Nor' Loch (which, when drained, became Princes Street Gardens).

Canonmills and Duddingston Loch were famous curling settings and the old Duddingston Society is the best-known local club in the annals of the game. In 1802, the Club instituted a silver medal, probably the first badge ever worn by curlers,* 'to distinguish the members from other gentlemen,' and, in 1809, originated the Points Competition – with three Points, Drawing, Striking and Inwicking – which the Currie Club enlarged to the system now in general use. The Club also went further than any other Club in collecting historical data and curling songs and verses.

But easily the greatest curling contribution made by the Duddingston Society was the framing of Rules which earned for Duddingston the proud title of 'the most influential local club in curling history'.

* Clubs all over the world now have their own Club badges, or 'pins' as they are called in Canada and the United States. Badges are exchanged during overseas tours, and on many other occasions, and curlers display their collections in show cases and under glass table tops. Fanatical collectors boast of a store of well over 1,000 badges. The old and rare 'pins' are the most sought after.

With the growth of Clubs in the eighteenth and early nine-teenth centuries, it became clear that districts, towns and villages could not continue to play the game in haphazard fashion under local, even club Rules, and that there was a need for national regulations.

Duddingston led the way towards this goal with a remarkable document, framed in the Curlers' Hall, Duddingston, 'upon the 6th January, 1804'. It was called 'Rules in Curling' and here it is in full :

I. The usual length of a rink is from thirty-six to forty-four yards inclusive; but this will be regulated by circumstances and the agreement of parties. When a game is begun the rink is not to be changed or altered, unless by the consent of the majority of players; nor is it to be shortened, unless it clearly appears that the majority are unable to make up.

II. The hog score to be one-sixth part of the length of the rink distant from the tee, and every stone to be deemed a hog the sole of which does not clear the score.

III. Each player to foot in such a manner that, in delivering his stone, he brings it over the tee.

IV. The order of playing adopted at the beginning must be observed during the whole course of a game.

V. All curling-stones to be of a circular shape. No stone is to be changed throughout a game, unless it happens to be broken; and the largest fragment of such stone to count, without any necessity of playing with it more. If a stone rolls or is upset, it must be placed upon its sole where it stops. Should a handle quit a stone in the delivery, the player must keep hold of it, otherwise he will not be entitled to replay the shot.

VI. A player may sweep his own stone the whole length of the rink; his party not to sweep until it has passed the hog score at the farther end, and his adversaries not to sweep until it has passed the tee. The sweeping to be always to a side.

VII. None of the players, upon any occasion, to cross or go upon the middle of the rink.

VIII. If in sweeping or otherwise a running stone is marred by any of the party to which it belongs, it must be put off the ice; if by any of the adverse party, it must be placed agreeable to the direction which was given to the player; and if it is marred by any other means, the player may take his shot again. Should a stone at rest be accidentally displaced, it must be put as nearly as possible to its former situation.

IX. Every player to be ready when his turn comes, and to take no more than a reasonable time to play his shot. Should he, by mistake, play with a wrong stone, it must be replaced where it stops by the one with which he ought to have played.

X. A doubtful shot is to be measured by some neutral person whose determination shall be final.

XI. Before beginning to play, each party must name one of their number for directing their game. The players of his party may give their advice to the one so named, but they cannot control his direction, nor are they to address themselves to the person who is about to play. Each director, when it is his turn to play, to name one of his party to take the charge for him. Every player to follow the direction given to him.

XII. Should any question arise the determination of which may not be provided for by the words and spirit of the rules now established, each party to choose one of their number in order to determine it. If the two so chosen differ in opinion, they are to name an umpire, whose decision shall be final.

These early Rules are remarkable not only for their solid commonsense but also because they bear a striking resemblance to the Rules in use today.

In particular, the following sections should be compared with the modern wording, shown later in this volume: 'The order of playing adopted at the beginning must be observed during the whole course of a game.' 'No stone is to be changed throughout a game, unless it happens to be broken; and the largest fragment of such stone to count, without any necessity of playing with it more. Should the handle quit a stone in the delivery, the player must keep hold of it, otherwise he will not be entitled to replay the shot.' 'If, in sweeping or otherwise, a running stone is marred by any of the party to which it belongs, it must be put off the ice; if by any of the adverse party, it must be placed agreeably to the direction which was given to the player.' 'Every player to be ready to play when his turn comes and to take no more than a reasonable time to play his shot.'

When the Grand Caledonian Curling Club, later to become the Royal Caledonian Curling Club, was formed in 1838, the new Club paid Duddingston the sincerest form of flattery by basing their Code of Rules on the Edinburgh Club's Rules. The fact that these old Rules have stood the test of time through 165 years is a tribute to the good sense and sagacity of the administrators whose Rules received 'the approbation and sanction of a general meeting of the Duddingston Curling Society' in 1804.

All curlers join the select group at that Meeting in acknowledging their debt to Duddingston. And let us also pay tribute to the Members of Rules Committees of the Royal Club through the years since 1838 for retaining the basic Rules, for striving always for simplicity – the keynote of legislation – and for refusing to be steam-rollered into widespread and needless Rules changes.

Prior to the formation of the 'Grand Caledonian', the organisation of big bonspiels had become increasingly difficult. At the matches between Midlothian and Peebles (1823) and Midlothian and Lanarkshire (1831), the sides could not agree about the Rules, the size of stones and the composition of rinks. It was reported: 'there was a want of co-operation between the players'. In 1834, an attempt to form an Amateur Curling Club of Scotland – with, among other distinguished office-bearers, the Ettrick Shepherd as one of its Secretaries – proved abortive. The curlers of Scotland were slow to act, and, ironically, when a Meeting was finally called, it very nearly broke up in disorder.

Despite claims from various parts of the country to the contrary, it is still uncertain who placed this advertisement in the North British Advertiser of 26th May, 1838 :*

'To Curlers. – In consequence of what is suggested at p. 11 of the *'Laws in Curling'* (a pamphlet just published by Maclachlan & Stewart, Edinburgh), it is hoped that the Initiated Curling Clubs in Scotland will depute one of the Brethren of their Court to meet in the Waterloo Hotel, Edinburgh, on Wednesday, the 20th June next, at 11 o'clock a.m., for the purpose of making the mysteries more uniform in future, and, if requisite, to form a Grand Court, to which all provincial ones shall be subject, and to elect a Grand President, with other Office-bearers. It is hoped that all Brethren who see this notice will direct the attention of their President or Secretary to it without delay. – 16th May 1838.'

A dozen curlers assembled at the Waterloo Hotel. It quickly became evident that the author of the advertisement was not present and the company split into uncertain little groups. Without a lead, without an agenda, no one knew where to start and the Meeting seemed about to disintegrate. At this psychological moment, a dapper one-armed figure entered, presented his card and announced himself, 'in a blunt, off-hand but frank and genial manner', as Mr Cairnie of Curling Hall.

He brought books which he had written on pond-making and other aspects of curling. The magnetism of his personality so impressed the Meeting that, although no one knew him personally, he was unanimously elected Chairman.

John Cairnie, born in Denny about 1769, inventor of artificial pond-making and of the foot-iron, which lasted for 100 years in Scottish curling, was a 'bonnie little man', a first-class curler,

---

* In his book, *Curling, The Ancient Scottish Game* (1884), the Rev. James Taylor wrote: 'There can be little or no doubt that Mr Cairnie was the author of the anonymous advertisement and that the lateness of his appearance at the Meeting was owing to the tediousness of a journey across the country from Largs.' This seemed eminently logical but Cairnie later stated that he was not the author (Royal Club *Annual*, 1844).

a benefactor to needy causes and a general favourite. He lost his left arm in a gunpowder explosion but this scarcely restricted his activities in his yacht or on the curling rink. After service as a surgeon in the East India Company and at sea, he settled in Largs, Ayrshire, in 1813, and built Curling Hall (now a Hotel) where he hoisted a banner on a high flagpole when curling was possible on his pond. He died in 1842 and his friend, Captain Paterson, wrote an elegy in his memory:

> 'Why droops the banner half-mast high,
> And curlers heave the bitter sigh?
> Why throughout Largs the tearful eye,
> So blear'd and red?
> Oh! listen to the poor man's cry!
> John Cairnie's dead!

> 'While winter's breath as waters freeze,
> Lays waste the fields and bares the trees,
> Or well-rigged yachts in joyous breeze
> For prizes ply,
> Cairnie! thy name by land or seas
> Shall never die.'

Cairnie's dramatic intervention saved the day and he guided the first perilous steps of the new national body. The Meeting came to order and resolved to issue another advertisement, under Cairnie's name, in three editions of the same newspaper, reporting the findings of the Members at the Meeting and adding: 'But, anxious for a fuller representation of the different Clubs throughout the country, in order to perpetuate and connect more closely the brotherhood in this ancient national game, they adjourned to Wednesday, 25th of July* next, at twelve o'clock in the Waterloo Hotel, when they hope the different Clubs of Scotland will make a point of sending deputations.'

This second Meeting, attended by representatives of 36 Clubs,

* To this day, the Annual Meeting of the Royal Caledonian Curling Club is held on the Wednesday nearest to 25th July.

was a complete success. Dr Renton of Penicuik proposed that the Grand Caledonian Curling Club, to be composed of the initiated Scottish Clubs, be instituted. This was agreed and Cairnie was unanimously elected President and James Skelton, W.S., of the Kinross Club, Secretary. A Committee was formed to consider regulations, mysteries and ceremonies and to prepare a mode of initiation and a set of Rules and Regulations.

The representatives met as strangers in the morning. Later in the day, a Curlers' Court was constituted by John Wright Williamson, Kinross, with the ancient ceremony for which he and the Kinross Club are famous. At a dinner in the evening, the Members greeted each other as brothers and were loath to part. It was the perfect example of the fellowship of curling and augured well for the future of the game's first national association.

The Club was soon to become international, but, first, it was to be honoured by Royal patronage – christened, as it were, by The Queen, and properly launched to serve not only on Scottish waters but in many parts of the world.

In 1842, the Earl of Mansfield, then President, entertained Queen Victoria and the Prince Consort at Scone Palace and presented to Prince Albert a pair of curling stones 'made of the finest Ailsa Craig granite, most beautifully finished and ornamented', with silver handles.* The Prince immediately accepted an invitation to become the first Patron of the Club.

After the presentation, Queen Victoria asked the Earl of Mansfield for details of curling and the Earl gave a demonstration of the game on the oak floor of the Palace ballroom, stones being thrown along the polished surface. The Queen herself threw a stone, understandably 'hogged' it and expressed surprise when told the length of a normal rink.

* We recall two other important presentations of curling stones. In 1867, a pair of stones, of fine Peebles porphyry, were sent by William Chambers, the Lord Provost of Edinburgh, to the Paris International Exhibition, and, at the end of the Exhibition, were presented to Emperor Napoleon III; and, in 1964, the Council of the Royal Club presented a beautiful pair of Red Hone Ailsas, suitably inscribed, to the Duke of Edinburgh, after the Duke's installation as President of the Royal Club.

In the following year, 1843, the 'Grand Caledonian' became the 'Royal Grand Caledonian'. Permission was quickly granted to drop the superfluous 'Grand' and the Royal Caledonian Curling Club was established.

Today, in a bookcase in the office of the Secretary of the Royal Club, a complete library of *Annuals* (Year Books) from the year 1839 forms an impressive record of the Club's meteoric rise from an association of 28 local Clubs to the world-wide organisation now called the 'Mother Club of Curling'.

In 1833, John Cairnie expressed the wish that all Scottish Clubs should correspond 'and give in a list of their office-bearers, the number of curlers, matches played and any matter connected with the game that was interesting'. This is, basically, what the *Annual* is. In addition, the book now contains details of all Overseas Associations and Clubs affiliated to the Royal Club and a section, recently introduced, composed of reports from all curling countries. The *Annual* has been called 'the curler's Bible' and it is certainly required reading for all 'converted' curlers and for those keen to start the game. The book also contains a full report of the Annual Meeting of the Club, a spread of photographs and . . . Get hold of a copy and read it for yourself!

Once started, the Royal Club took firm root. The number of affiliated Scottish Clubs almost doubled in two years, more than trebled in three years and quadrupled to 116 Clubs in five years. The first edition of the *Annual* – containing a recommendation to use Cairnie's foot-iron, a plea to equalise the weights and sizes of curling stones and a request to Clubs 'to contribute such funds as they may think proper' in the first year of management – ran to only 300 copies.

Now, in addition to the 600 British Clubs affiliated to the Royal Club, many thousands of overseas Clubs are affiliated through their national Associations; and the *Annual* is circulated to each British Club and to fourteen countries overseas.

A Member of the Royal Family was Patron of the Royal Club each year from the date of its inception until 1900. When Edward VII succeeded to the throne, he became the first King to be Patron, and, since then, the Patron has been The King or The Queen.

The Prince of Wales was elected President in 1925, the Duke of Edinburgh in 1964, and, through the years, distinguished Presidents, famous in many walks of Scottish life, have served the Royal Club. The post has become much more onerous in recent years, entailing a busy round of meetings, functions of all types and tours overseas. The reason is simple : the Royal Club has kept abreast with the tremendous upsurge in curling interest since the Second War and, indeed, has led the way in many of the exciting moves (described later in this book) brought about by the curling boom throughout the world.

Similarly, the Members of the Royal Club Council give, willingly and at their own expense, more and more of their time and energy for love of the game and the fellowship it engenders. The wide, and ever-widening, range of curling activities demands additional sub-committees,* thought, imagination and hard work each year.

In 1966, the Club purchased premises at 2 Coates Crescent, Edinburgh, and thus became the owner of Headquarters for the first time. All Royal Club Secretaries have been based in Edinburgh and it is interesting to note that the present Secretary, whose 14-foot long boardroom table is covered with correspondence from many lands, is only the eighth man to hold the post since 1838 – a remarkable record, particularly since the first Secretary, James Skelton, held the position for two years and the second, George Ritchie, just one year more.†

* Among the recent Committees formed by the Royal Club are an International Committee (which is self-explanatory) and an Extension Committee (which has prepared a File to help those interested in building an Ice Rink).

† Three Secretaries served the Royal Club for a span of exactly 100 years – Alex. Cassels, W.S., (33 years from 1843 to 1876); A. Davidson Smith, C. A., (40 years from 1880 to 1920); and Andrew H. Hamilton, S.S.C., whose son James followed him for 11 years, (27 years from 1920 to 1947).

CHAPTER EIGHT

THE GRAND MATCH

EASILY THE MOST spectacular Royal Club event – if it comes off – is the Grand Match between the North and South of Scotland on outside ice. The 'Nation's Bonspiel' is a magnificent sight with 600 rinks of Scots curlers fighting it out in friendly rivalry on a major Scottish loch. The Match, the biggest bonspiel in the world, takes precedence over all other competitions because, under the Constitution of the Royal Club, 'all matches must give place to the Grand Match'.

But six inches of good black ice are needed for the Match and too often the planning undertaken by the dedicated Members of the Grand Match Committee is in vain. Each year, the Match is planned, down to the last detail, by fifty keen curlers. It is a labour of love. Three venues are possible – Loch Leven in Kinross, the Lake of Menteith near Stirling or Lindores Loch near Newburgh in Fife – and the one which offers the best conditions under hard frost is chosen.

The present Convener of the Grand Match Committee, William Murray of Glenfarg,* has co-ordinated and inspired the efforts for the big Bonspiel for more than a dozen years and all curlers who have enjoyed a Grand Match or who look forward to one are indebted to him. Each year, he presides, with his own brand of native wit, at two official Meetings, first to make the draw for the Match, from entries which pour in from Clubs in early summer. At this Meeting, a demarcation line dividing

* When a group of Scots travelled to Montreal in March 1968 to attend the World Championship for the Air Canada Silver Broom, they flew over Greenland. Looking down at the superb view of ice fields and glaciers, Lord Bruce, now the Earl of Elgin, the Royal Club President, remarked: 'What a paradise for Willie Murray!'

North and South is cunningly drawn; each group of entries affects this 'sliding line' but an amicable decision is always reached and 300 teams are placed on the North side, 300 on the South.

In October or November each year, Willie Murray also takes the chair at a large-scale Meeting of the Grand Match Committee, at which all aspects of the comprehensive preparatory work are carefully delegated to active sub-committees. Every section of the work, from ice-making and car-parking to flagpoles and latrines, is placed in responsible hands.

The organisation is in the nature of a military operation, in which a highly-proficient corps of men, led by Willie Murray, make everything ready for the final command from General Jack Frost. The 'Match-On' signal, relayed by the B.B.C. the night before the big day, is the climax to months of preparation. Only those actively involved in the preliminary work can fully appreciate the build-up necessary for the greatest Bonspiel in the world.

> They come frae glens at John o' Groats,
> And south frae Gallowa',
> And eastward frae the Neuk o' Fife
> And west frae dark Loch Awe.
>
> The day has dawned, the tees are marked,
> The crampits pointed fairly,
> The cannon booms, the besoms wave,
> The combat opens rarely.
>
> Jas. Christie, Dollar, 1867.

The last two Grand Matches, on Loch Leven in 1959 and the Lake of Menteith in 1963, amply repaid the Grand Match Committee for long periods of hard work and frustration. As a starting signal, a cannon is fired* and 2,400 curlers from all

---

* A six-pounder gun, captured at the siege of Acre in 1779 and gifted to the Royal Club by Sir John Ogilvie in 1853, was used to start Grand Matches. Unfortunately, this gun has been lost.

parts of Scotland engage in a three-hour battle on rinks feverishly marked out by the Ice Committee on the previous two days. The marking is carried out by skilled men who use 'tee-ringers' – boards with nails inserted – and iron pencils to scrape circles and lines on the ice. These specialists must accomplish their task, to mark 300 sheets of ice for play, in two days; if they take longer, a thaw may come and the chance of holding the Match could well be lost. (The Grand Match entry is now limited to 600 rinks for this reason).

There are various types of ice. Only two concern us – transparent or black ice; white, opaque or snow ice. Black ice, the type needed for a Grand Match, is the result of frost on a sheet of still water. Although actually colourless and transparent, it appears to be black or dark-green. This is by far the safest type of ice.

White ice is produced when snow is partially melted and then congealed on the ice or when snow falls while the first frost crystals are formed on the water. Being full of air bubbles, white ice is dangerous and not to be trusted.

The first Grand Match was held at Penicuik, a few miles from Edinburgh, on 15th January, 1847. The Match, twelve-rinks -a-side, was played in the grounds of Sir George Clerk, Bt., who, in 1839, had become the second Royal Club President, and the painting of the occasion is owned by the present Baronet, Sir John Clerk of Penicuik House. A spectator in 1847 reported that 'the day throughout was one of unmingled pleasure, and, saving the absence of a barrel of exhilarating ale, which was unfortunately omitted among the items of preparation, there was nothing but universal satisfaction felt and expressed'.

The second Grand Match, on Linlithgow Loch in 1848, attracted a bigger entry – 280 curlers competing compared with 96 at Penicuik the year before. The increase was moderate, predictable. But the Match at Linlithgow, the subject of a well-known painting by Charles Lees, R.S.A., had far-reaching effects.

More than 6,000 people came to watch and many of them congregated in large groups round the play. Among others, Sir

John Ogilvy, later to become President of the Royal Club, left the Loch contemplating the consequences of similar support at future Grand Matches. Sir John's fears prompted him to propose, at the Royal Club Meeting in 1851, 'that the Royal Club should have a piece of ground which could be flooded for the purpose of affording a safe sheet of ice for the Grand Matches'.

This led Mrs Home Drummond Stirling Moray of Abercairney to grant permission to use her land at Carsebreck – between Greenloaning and Blackford, near Gleneagles in Perthshire – at a rent of £15 for 63 acres from November to February each season. The area was flooded, and, from 1853 to 1935, 25 Grand Matches were played at Carsebreck. To begin with, the deepest point was five feet, nine inches, but, before the Second World War, the level of water had risen to seven or eight feet, and, because the pond was solid with weeds, it was described as a 'white elephant'.

The last Match there, on 24th December, 1935, was the biggest ever held – 2,576 curlers enjoying the day's play despite the fact that a sudden thaw ruined the final hour on the ice, rain started to fall and the players finished 'up to the fetlocks in water'!

One of the rinks of the winning Club in 1935, Monzievaird and Strowan, won by 46 shots to 2. Other runaway victories were 44–5, 39–10, 36–6, 34–3 and 30–2. One rink, which shall remain nameless, was 'soutered' – the name taken from an invincible team of Lochmaben shoemakers, or souters, at the end of the eighteenth century – 23–0. On the same ice, there were two drawn games, 21–21 and 6–6.

Such wide scoring variations are common at Grand Matches which have also produced the three most sensational results in the long history of the game. Donald Fisher, Dunkeld, in 1855, and John Laurie, Bute, in 1867, scored only one shot each but won their games; and, in 1853, Alexander Cunningham of the Currie Club recorded a 71–1 victory. The remarks of his wretched opponents are not recorded!

The only other outdoor venue was Lochwinnoch (1850 and

1864), and, in all, 37 Grand Matches have been played since 1847, 32 of them on outside ice, of which one was played in November, nine were played in December, sixteen in January and six in February. The other five Matches were held indoors in the Edinburgh and Glasgow Ice Rinks, in order to defeat the vagaries of Jack Frost, and there have been recent suggestions to repeat the experiment. However well-intentioned, such proposals miss the whole point of the operation and we hope they will not be pursued. A Grand Match in an Ice Rink is, surely, a contradiction in terms.

The organisation of today's Grand Match Committee is so highly geared that every possible chance of holding the Match out of doors is explored – to make the possibility, under continuing frost, a probability, eventually a reality. Excerpts from the Diary of the Convener, Willie Murray, for 'Operation Grand Match 1963', prove the point:

9th January, 1963. – Met James Hamilton (Ice Vice-Convener) and Sir David Montgomery (Ice Convener). Convener handed over his detailed list of duties and instructions, with powers to employ the boatmen at Loch Leven and his farm manager for haulage of equipment for marking off ice, and snow scoops and shovels.

10th January. – James Hamilton inspected Lake of Menteith. Only about $\frac{1}{2}''$ of snow on good black ice. Too much snow and rough ice at Loch Leven and Lindores Loch.

11th January. – James Hamilton reported to Royal Club Secretary and Convener for warning post-cards to go out on 12th January.

Saturday, 12th January. – James Hamilton made arrangements to go to Lake of Menteith the next day with equipment for marking rinks and clearing snow and to take Tom Stark and J. Sneddon. Asked R. Keay to have 6 additional snow scrapers ready as soon as possible, and some iron pencils.

Sunday, 13th January. – Went to Lake of Menteith with marking gear. Met local Ice Committee; also the Royal Club President Gilbert McClung and Secretary Robin Welsh, from

Edinburgh. Had been more snow now, about $\frac{3}{4}''$, but there was 5" of good black ice below. All agreed everything should be set going for Wednesday. If a good weather report on Tuesday, then Robin Welsh to be notified and B.B.C. announcement put over for 6 p.m. news bulletin. Tom Stark demonstrated marking off of rinks to local helpers and arranged for marking the next day.

Monday, 14th January. – James Hamilton took David Montgomery's two men and proceeded to mark off and clear the snow off rinks as marked. 115 rinks completed. More help required to finish. James Hamilton and convener arranged for 12 additional men from Orwell and Glenfarg Clubs.

Tuesday, 15th January, 7.50 a.m. – Meteorological forecast for 48 hours: some snow but with 4° of frost, and snow to come overnight. Set off in car from Glenfarg for Lake of Menteith to make the final assessment with Ice Committee and to take ice thickness. James Hamilton met me on ice and got an ice measurement of 6", with various others about $5\frac{1}{2}''$. Weather overcast. Called Ice Committee together. Gave them weather forecast from Pitreavie. Ice up to 6" with frost at night and under influence of high pressure system. All agreed to call the match. Telephoned Edinburgh and that brought Robin Welsh in to undertake his multifarious duties. Extra men helped to finish marking off and clearing rings of snow. Extra clearing shovels all needed. Put out wood blocks for numbering rinks. Parking Committee Convener, Col. J. R. Buchanan, held meeting of Committee with A. D. Callander and others with Police Chief Davidson from Dunblane and Inspector McRae and A.A. representative. Convener put up all notices and coloured direction signs. Radio and T.V. cameras and teams arrived. Sandy Callander met Robin Welsh in Stirling.

Convener and Secretary interviewed by Radio and T.V. authorities who gave us great support and coverage. Did not finish with the T.V. men till about midnight. Sandy and Robin wrote out and headed 450 scoring cards after that and finished and got to bed 2.45 a.m. During this operation, the writing hands got very cramped and had to get treated and relieved by the Convener and mine host at intervals with coffee, tea and John Barleycorn to finish off. During the marking of the cards, roaring cracks were heard from the Lake, but Sandy assured us that was a sign that the frost was catching and the ice settling. Although there was no frost in the evening, by the time we went home from the Hotel the frost had materialised and everything was hard. All much relieved.

Wednesday, 16th January. – Robin and I got up 7 a.m. Put the number of the rinks on Parking Plans. Breakfasted at 8 a.m. Arrived Lake Hotel 8.45 a.m. Six policemen and the Inspector on the job. Snowing! Showed the Police the layout and gave them all parking plans which had been prepared by Col. J. R. Buchanan. (Coloured car labels guide curlers to their parking section – conveniently near the rink on which they will play). Cleared equipment from front of Hotel for cannon and loud-speaker. James Hamilton arrived with Loch Leven men to put on numbers. Still snowing, could not put up flags on roof flag pole. Sent R. Paterson to assist putting numbers on rinks. James Hamilton brought through six plans of layout of rinks prepared by R. Dalziel, David Montgomery's factor. He surveyed the rinks the day before and had all ready for J. Hamilton at 8 a.m. at Blairnathort. Windows in Hotel lounge were used for 'North' and 'South' cards and a plan and the draw was displayed on a tree outside the Hotel. Cars, buses, and the curlers and stones began to arrive and everything went smoothly. Weather cleared and sun shone. Andrew Oswald's bus for people off train at Stirling well filled. Brigadier Gow's cannon arrived in good time with Mr Campbell his Forester and was duly set off by the Secretary at noon to start play, the President having welcomed everyone over the loudspeaker and the Secretary having read message to The Queen and read out The Queen's gracious reply.

During the match, a herd of Red Deer were seen on the horizon, coming down from the Trossachs over the hill, first of all in single file, then spreading out as they came down. The lovely setting was admired by everyone. I will treasure very happy memories of the whole occasion and all who helped to make the great 'day'.

All Scots curlers should play in a Grand Match and should
respond to Willie Murray's call to come in something tartan, if
only a ribbon round a balmoral. In *The Complete Curler* (1914),
Gordon Grant says of the Match: 'there is nothing like it in
the wide world'. It starts at noon and ends at 3 p.m., exactly
as at Penicuik in 1847. An essentially Scottish experience, the
Grand Match is a national institution.

CHAPTER NINE

THE GROWTH OF ARTIFICIAL ICE RINKS

THERE IS EVIDENCE that Scottish curlers, in revolt against their treatment by the weather, discussed the possibility of playing on an artificial surface in the early years of the nineteenth century. But the first *concrete* move was made by the irrepressible John Cairnie, whose book, *Essay on Curling and Artificial Pond Making,* was published in 1833.

More than 20 years before this, Cairnie suggested to the Duddingston Curling Society, of which he was a member, that artificial ponds should be laid. He started to build a pond but abandoned the idea when he could not find anyone to help him to finance the project. Thoughts of his pond would not leave him, and, after a Duddingston Club dinner in Edinburgh in 1827, he resolved to make a clay pond at his own expense. The pond, built on his land at Curling Hall, Largs, was completed early in January, 1828, and, on 11th January, 'after one night's frost, a party of eight gentlemen had the satisfaction of enjoying curling on it in all its perfection'.*

Cairnie constructed his clay pond with small nodules of whinstone pounded into the clay and claimed that almost half of his pond 'exhibited a surface of stone'. He emphasised that the surface had to be level and that, when flooded to the depth of a quarter of an inch, it provided ice after one night's frost.

Cairnie hoped that this pond, which could be made at a trifling cost, would be used in Scots parishes. His paved rink,

* The Rev. J. Somerville of Currie also claimed the invention and there was much controversy, and acrimonious correspondence, on the subject. It appears to us that Cairnie's claim was fair since his pond was *artificial* while Somerville's had a *natural* base.

the idea for which sprang from youthful memories of making ice on pavements, 'to the great annoyance of His Majesty's lieges,' was much more expensive; 46 yards long and six yards broad at the ends, the 20-yard centre section being narrower, only four yards wide. On a base of lime and gravel mixed with gravel and sea sand, four-and-a-half-inch pavement stones were laid, with bevelled kerbs at the edges of the rink so that stones struck against them would run off the pond without damage. Masons were instructed to dress each pavement stone to a perfect level; Cairnie claimed that the greatest deviation from the level on his pond did not exceed a quarter of an inch. The freestone 'flags' were then flooded with a few gallons of water from a force pump and curling was possible with reasonable frost although the rink was little more than 100 yards from the sea.

Cairnie's invention was adopted and improved by Clubs throughout the nineteenth century. Concrete, asphalt and other bases were used but the principle was the same – the laying of a non-porous surface, which, when flooded, provided ice under a few degrees of frost.

The movement was carried a stage further through the genius of John Loudon Macadam (1756–1836), the Scot who invented the tarmacadam system of road-making. No curling history would be complete without a tribute to tarmac, which popularised curling throughout Scotland nearly 70 years ago.

The first tarmac curling rinks, the forerunners of hundreds in the country, were laid in Edinburgh in 1902 by the Watsonian Curling Club. The rinks, now lost to view under a rebuilding scheme at Watson's College Playing Fields at Myreside, were laid by Andrew Scott, the Myreside groundsman, who offered his services to other curling clubs in an advertisement in Josh Bowie's treatise, *The Art of the Game* (1904). The tarmac rink soon superseded the concrete rinks which had a tendency to crack and develop bumps. Another reason for the sudden popularity of tarmac was the cost. A concrete curling rink cost over £100 while a tarmac rink could be laid for £20 or £30.

But the greatest advantage of tarmac was the reduction of preparatory work and the frequency of play. On many concrete

Top Left: The oldest known stone, the Stirling Stone, with another ancient stone (*bottom left*) in the Smith Institute, Stirling. The Jubilee Stone (*right*), the heaviest stone in existence (117 pounds) is included in the Royal Club's exhibition of curling relics in the Perth Ice Rink. *Below:* These old trickers are also on display in Perth Ice Rink. At back is a stoup – a tankard used for collecting fines at Curlers' Courts – and a wooden 'Bottle' or 'Dolly' still used on the Continent and Scandinavia to mark the 'Tee' (centre of the circles)

Bill Robertson Aikman of the Hamilton and Thornyhill Club (*above left*) throws a stone from the wooden hack made by his father Col Robertson Aikman. This forerunner of the modern hack has a semi-circular hole cut in the wood, into which the foot is set at an angle. The shape of the cut-out portion is similar to the hole cut in the ice by old-time Sanquhar curlers. *Right and below*: Willie Young, famous Scottish skip, shows his unusual delivery action. He lines up the shot on the crampit with the handle of the stone at the same angle for in-hand and out-hand. At the end of his delivery, he slides forward on his right foot (the 'wrong' foot in the conventional delivery). Willie Young's Club is Airth, Bruce Castle and Dunmore

and other shallow ponds, water lying up to an inch deep required a hard frost before play was possible. On tarmac, only a light spray of water was needed with the temperature a degree or two below freezing point and the game was on.

As the tarmac revolution swept the country, curling clubs vied with each other in providing efficient lighting systems for their ponds. Previously, as twilight merged into night, white handkerchiefs were dangled on skips' brooms and candles, lanterns and flares were lit in an effort to prolong the play.*

The new systems of lighting changed the complexion of club activities. Naphtha, paraffin, acetylene and gas, with electricity the crowning amenity, illuminated the Scottish scene, and, providing for evening and late night play, doubled the amount of curling.† (Some clubs which did not have their own ponds, negotiated with tennis clubs so that, with a water supply readily available, curling could be played on the courts in winter).

George Harris, Secretary of the Arbroath Curling Club, wrote in 1910: 'Before this improvement (tarmac), our club could only get a game during very hard frost, but, this season, we enjoyed the pleasures of the roarin' game on forty different occasions, the most interesting games being played in the evenings under electric light.'‡

* In more recent times, we have heard of outdoor curling being played at nights under the glare of the headlamps of cars suitably stationed round a loch or pond.

† The most ingenious lighting system we have heard of was constructed, on what was called the Model Curling Pond, by Major Henderson, President of Bridge of Allan Curling Club, at Westerton, near Bridge of Allan, over 100 years ago. Round the pond, Major Henderson, the proprietor, set up lines of lanterns which were attached by gutta-percha tubes to an underground gas pipe which supplied Bridge of Allan. Using the same source of power, the Major lit the pathway leading from the town to the pond with lanterns hanging from a row of trees.

‡ A sheet of polythene laid on an existing pond holds water well and is much cheaper than making repairs to the pond. The Earl of Elgin, President of the Royal Club from 1967 to 1969, laid polythene on his pond at Broomhall, Dunfermline, last season, and reported that the ice had been good for curling.

Tarmac gave a fresh impetus to curling in Scotland and literally paved the way towards the advent of the big indoor Ice Rinks.

INDOOR RINKS :

Early attempts to build indoor Ice Rinks proved abortive and it was a long time before indoor Rinks were properly established and curlers could say with the versifier :

> Fare thee well, O fickle frost,
> Thou'rt no more the curler's boast.

The first attempt, made by a Mr Henry Kirk in London as early as 1842, was described in the Royal Club *Annual* of that year : 'A new marvellous feat of science is added to those by which this era has been already distinguished, in the discovery of a chemical compound having all the appearance of ice – capable of being deposited in the sheet, and offering to the skater a surface much more agreeable for the purposes of his graceful exercise than that ordinarily supplied by the winter operations of nature upon our park waters. The gentleman who has achieved this victory over the elements of chemistry, Mr Henry Kirk, now exhibits the results of his five years' labour to that end, at a building on the grounds of Mr Jenkins in the New Road near to Dorset Square. The floor of an apartment there is covered with an apparently icy integument – not quite as clear as crystal but like congelation after a white frost – upon which a considerable number of members of the skating club indulged in their evolutions. This substance, seven-eighths of an inch thick, cannot be broken by any concussion short of that by a sledge-hammer.'

The reaction of curlers of the time was cool and critical : 'We know not whether artificial ice can be made available to the purposes of curling. To the really useful ends of curling, considered as a winter amusement to the rural part of the population disengaged from labour, artificial ice cannot be of much advantage.'

Mr Kirk's building, 70 feet long by 50 feet wide, was called a Glaciarium. It did not last, and, as far as we know, curling was never played there, but the seed had been planted. There *was* curling in the Rusholme Rink in Manchester in 1877, on ice processed by Professor Gamgee, whose Secretary, Mr Hyde, travelled to Scotland, with a file of testimonials, in an attempt to set up Ice Rinks in Edinburgh and Glasgow. But nothing further was heard of the project.

The cost of the Rink, £20,000, seems excessive in that Mid-Victorian period, but the next Glaciarium, built on the Gamgee principle and opened in Southport in 1879, cost over £30,000.* Edward Holden presented the Holden Challenge Shield, value 50 guineas, for competition twice a year, and the event was played at Southport until 1889. The Shield is now the prize for the Royal Club Rink Championship, a competition open to rinks of four Regular Members of the same Club, which annually attracts an entry of over 400 rinks.

The Royal Club held its Annual Meeting in Southport in 1885, in recognition of the services given to curling by the Glaciarium, and, after the Meeting, the Mayor of Southport welcomed over 200 curlers in the Prince of Wales Hotel. But the Rink went into liquidation in 1890 with a loss of £25,000, most of which was borne by Edward Holden.

Referring to the failure of the Rink, in the curling section of *The Badminton Library* (1892), the Rev. John Kerr skated on thin ice, which has since given way under him, when he prophesied. 'As the Southport Rink has had to be closed for want of patronage, it is to be feared that the chances of any further development of this ice-making scheme are very small.'

It was fitting that, when the cannie Scots at last decided to follow the example of their brother curlers in England, their in-door Ice Rinks, after a hesitant start, should take firm root. It was also natural because the curling population was already there, eagerly looking for outlets for more play.

---

* The Southport Glaciarium Cup is now played for annually by the Preston and Dalbeattie Clubs.

The first indoor Ice Rink in Scotland was the Scottish Ice Rink, at Crossmyloof in Glasgow, opened on 1st October, 1907. A small group of business men formed a private company and launched a new era in Scottish curling.

The Scottish Ice Rink Skating and Curling Pavilion had a bandstand high up in the centre of the Rink, an idea derived from the Moulin Rouge in Paris. The Rink contained 'a dining-room, smoking room, kitchen and *what not*', and 'spectator learners' were encouraged to curl on vacant ice in the evenings at a very modest fee. The Rink lasted until 1917 and the existing Scottish Ice Rink – which, with seventeen curling sheets, is Europe's largest Ice Rink – was built on the ruins of the old Pavilion in 1928.

The 4-sheet Lochrin Ice Pond at Tollcross, Edinburgh, was the next indoor Rink. Opened in January, 1912, it was the home of the Edinburgh Corporation, Edinburgh Markets and Edinburgh Masonic Clubs and promised well but the venture was short-lived.

The much bigger Edinburgh Ice Rink, at Haymarket, Edinburgh, is the oldest existing Rink in Scotland. Opened on 5th February, 1912, by Lord Balfour of Burleigh, it was, when the old Scottish Ice Rink failed, the only Ice Rink in Scotland, and, for many years, curlers from all parts of the country came to Edinburgh for their major bonspiels, Provincial Matches and challenge games.

An Ice Rink in Aberdeen – the Aberdeen Winter Recreation Institute in Forbesfield Road – was opened in September, 1912, but closed its doors in 1917 and Aberdonian curlers have used another setting, Donald's Ice Rink, for the last 20 years, the building having been converted from a garage to a skating rink in 1939. Ice Rink building in Scotland then lapsed, until, in the mid-thirties, the sister winter sport of ice-hockey gave curlers a helping hand and the game itself the fillip it needed to enter the modern era. The sudden boom of ice-hockey attracted business-men to build Ice Rinks, with accommodation for spectators, to satisfy the demand for the game. The boom days are over but the spectacular sport left a legacy

to the curling fraternity which curlers gratefully accepted before
the war and still acknowledge today.

The estimated cost of Perth Ice Rink (called the Central
Scotland Ice Rink) was £26,000, an interesting figure to lay
alongside the £30,000 expended at Southport almost 60 years
before. The Rink, which was opened by the Duke of Atholl on
1st October, 1936, offered many new amenities, including
seating for 2,000 spectators, and advertised 'The Haven'
tearoom – 'for Tea, Hot Muffins and a Chat'. Today, in the
spacious lounge bar, paintings and relics, on loan from the
Royal Club, are exhibited,

Kirkcaldy Ice Rink, Dundee-Angus Ice Rink in Dundee,
Falkirk Ice Rink and Dunfermline Ice Rink (which closed 14
years ago) all opened in 1938; and Ayr Ice Rink quickly followed, being officially launched on 13th March, 1939. The big
Murrayfield Ice Rink, in the grounds of the Scottish Rugby
Union in Edinburgh, was built in 1939 and became a war
casualty. It now concentrates on skating but offers three curling
sessions on Tuesdays and Thursdays during the season. Curling
was also played at Paisley Ice Rink just prior to and during the
Second World War but there has been no curling there since.

After the spate of Ice Rink building in the 'thirties, there
was a standstill for 25 years. The 'freeze' was eventually broken
by the singleminded purpose of W. D. Wilson of St Boswells, a
famous Border curler and an overseas tourist of repute. Willie
Wilson returned from Royal Club tours in Canada and the
United States determined to build an Ice Rink in the Borders,
a traditional stronghold of the game.

He gathered round him an energetic group of keen curlers
who were fired with his enthusiasm. A public meeting was held
in Kelso in January, 1963, and this led to the formation of the
Border Ice Rink Ltd., with Willie Wilson as Chairman. The
£40,000 four-sheet Rink, situated alongside Kelso Golf Club,
was opened on 1st October, 1964, and its success has exceeded
all expectations.

Before Willie Wilson's inspiration, the eight major Ice Rinks
in Scotland had been bursting at the seams, and it was clear

that expansion was vital, but extension meetings broke up in disorder when capital expenditure was mentioned. The Border Rink was the spur. Within four years, four new indoor Rinks made their appearance, the first of which, admittedly, was part of a massive new scheme and not a private venture.

The late Hugh Fraser, a restless Scots industrialist, was the driving force behind the Aviemore Centre, the £3,000,000 complex within which the luxurious Aviemore Ice Rink is a focal point. The Centre, in its beautiful setting in the Cairngorm Mountains, was opened on 14th December, 1966, and the Aviemore Ice Rink, the second largest in Britain, has been visited by curlers from many nations and is already a name to conjure with in the curling world.

A month later, on 20th January, 1967, the South of Scotland Ice Rink opened at Lockerbie in Dumfriesshire. The five-sheet Rink, with a design similar to the Border Ice Rink, on which it was based, is now one of the busiest Ice Rinks in the country – a resounding success which is giving valuable service particularly to the South of Scotland and the North of England.

The idea of the Lanarkshire Ice Rink at Hamilton was born in 1964 during a Canadian Tour by a Scottish Rotarian curling team, which included Tom Dickson, now Chairman of the Board. It was highly appropriate, therefore, that Jack McKimmie, Gerry Boyd, Doug Washer and Bill Miller from Lachute flew from Canada for the opening ceremony for it was at Lachute that a small group of curlers discussed designs and dreamed of a brand new Rink. The dream became a reality on 29th September, 1967, when the Rink was opened by Bill Robertson Aikman, Immediate Past-President of the Royal Club, an internationally famous curler and himself a Hamilton man.

The Inverness Ice Rink at Bught Park, Inverness, joined the growing number of Scottish Rinks in 1968. A five-sheet Rink with first-class amenities, it has attracted solid bookings and looks forward to a bright future.

The recent Ice Rink development programme has produced a remarkable paradox : as each new Ice Rink was launched, curlers wondered how it would prosper and how its bookings would affect the nearest existing Ice Rink; again, it was hoped that the new Rinks would ease the strain of excessive demands at the older Rinks and that orders for curling ice would be evenly spread throughout the country so that Clubs, whose requests for ice had been cut in recent years, could be given a fuller allocation of ice.

This has not happened for one simple reason: as new Rinks have sprung up, they have encouraged the formation of many new Clubs so that the curling population has kept in step with the increase in Ice Rinks, making the many Ice Rinks as busy as the few Ice Rinks were before.

A survey of the situation in the fourteen curling Rinks in Scotland prompts this considered opinion – that the country can easily support more Ice Rinks than at present and that many more Rinks will be built in the future.

It may be that advantage will be taken of the new plastic Rink, opened in Stockholm in December, 1967, which is the first indoor Rink of its kind in the world. A reinforced plastic cloth covering, which weighs three tons, is anchored in a concrete base weighing 250 tons and is kept up, even in the strongest wind, by two warm air fans. The air, 20,000 cubic metres per hour, is blown in through grids, does not inconvenience the players in any way and reduces the condensation to a minimum. The wholly automatic system is regulated by thermostats and an ideal temperature is maintained. The ice, which is formed through plastic pipes in a concrete floor, is pebbled.

The plastic stadium has two big advantages. In less than five days, the eight curling sheets in Stockholm can be converted to three tennis courts; and the construction costs are much less than for a conventional type building.

The situation in England is far less healthy. After the failure of the Southport Rink, there was curling at the Prince's Skating and Curling Club in London, and, on 27th October, 1910, the Manchester Ice Palace was opened. This was the venue for the small but vital group of Clubs which comprise the First English Province of the Royal Club – until 1962. Imagine the feelings of the curlers in the Province when the Ice Palace was taken over for other activities and curling in the area was lost!

What can a keen curler do when he suddenly finds he has no ice to play on? To their eternal credit, the English curlers – many of whom are Scots, or have Scots ancestry – did not give up or even contemplate giving up. They rearranged their programme, staged their principal bonspiel in Edinburgh, and carried out a series of raids over the Border to keep their hand in. The South of Scotland Ice Rink became an oasis for men thirsty for ice and Lockerbie now figures prominently on the Province fixture list.

The First English Province curlers, who have been called 'the keenest of the keen', have a long and strong curling tradition. The late Willie Kerr, known as 'the father of English Curling', was the embodiment of all that is good in the game. His sons, Edward and Dan, have worthily maintained that tradition, and they, with J. L. Kerr, other members of the Kerr family and a select band of real enthusiasts continue to preserve curling as a vital force with few of the benefits enjoyed by Scots curlers.

The Province at last obtained 'home ice' again four years ago by a lucky chance. The Manager of the Ice Drome at Blackpool, Tony Scott, saw Tom Kerr, Dan Kerr's son, skating on a Sunday in his Preston Curling Club sweater. Their meeting led to regular play at Blackpool where the rinks are a little short, but what matter – the game's the thing!

The only other Rink in England where curling is played regularly is the Richmond Ice Rink in Twickenham, London. The building was constructed by a Belgian company as a munitions factory during the First World War. The Richmond Ice Rink was founded in 1928, and, by strange coincidence, Ronald Alpe, who has been Manager at Richmond for over 30 years, first visited the site when it was a car components factory just prior to becoming an Ice Rink.

Two Scots, the late Harry Rule, C.A., and William C. Blair, who is still a keen and active curler, were prime movers in a drive which led to the formation of the Richmond Curling Club in 1951, Harry Rule becoming the first President. There are now

The two rinks which have carried Scotland's banner in world events in recent years. *Top:* Chuck Hay's rink of Perthshire farmers who won the World Championship in 1967 – from left, Chuck Hay (Skip), John Bryden (third), Alan Glen (second) and David Howie (lead). *Below:* Alex Torrance's rink from the Hamilton and Thornyhill Club who forced the Canadian champions under Lyall Dagg to an extra end in the final of the World Championship in Calgary in 1964. *From left*, Alex F. Torrance (Skip), Alex Torrance (third), Bobby Kirkland (second) and Jimmy Waddell (lead). Scotland's representatives, who came third in the 1969 World Championship, were Bill Muirhead (Skip), George Haggart, Derek Scott and Alex Young from Perth

Delivery actions of Chuck Hay and his rink taken at the top of the backswing, when the stone reached the ice and at the point of release. *From top:* Chuck Hay, John Bryden, Alan Glen and David Howie

seven Clubs in the Province of London and the members curl once a week, on a Tuesday evening, in a Rink which is world-famous as a skating centre.

An interesting fact emerged in conversation* after the Scotland *v*. England curling international at Richmond in 1968 : that, in pre-war days, an ice-making plant had been installed under the ballroom in London's exclusive Grosvenor House for skating and ice-hockey. There is no record of curling being played there, which is a pity. When asked, 'Where are you curling?' it would have been pleasant to answer – 'Oh, in Park Lane !'

* With Ronald Alpe.

CHAPTER TEN

HOW TO CURL

WHAT IS CURLING? The first historical description is still the best. Two hundred years ago, a non-curling English tourist called Pennant wrote a paragraph about the game in *A Tour in Scotland and Voyage to the Hebrides* (1772):

'Of the sports in these parts, that of Curling is a favourite and one unknown in England. It is an amusement of the winter, and played on the ice by sliding from one mark to another great stones of 40 to 70 pounds weight, of hemispherical form with an iron or wooden handle at top. The object of the player is to lay his stone as near to the mark as possible, to guard that of his partner, which had been well laid before, or to strike off that of his antagonist.' For simplicity and clarity, that last sentence cannot be bettered.

The game is played by two teams of four players, each using two stones and playing them alternately with his opponent. A curler throws 40-pound stones over 40 yards to circles marked on the ice, and often coloured. The playing of all sixteen stones constitutes an 'end' and the teams then play up the same ice in the opposite direction at the next end. The aim is to count more stones than your opponents nearer the centre of the circles (the tee) at the conclusion of each end.

There are many ways of achieving this, the most important being that you play better than the opposition and that you have the last stone, but, for the moment, let us assume that you are a complete beginner – man or woman, boy or girl – who has never played before. We will start from scratch, or, to use a more appropriate term, from rock bottom, and will formulate a plan of campaign to transform you from a beginner to an

74

average player, able to play your full part in a rink. The much more difficult transformation from an average to a first-class player is not within our province and is entirely up to you.

1. Go to your nearest Ice Rink and watch good curlers, preferably very good curlers, and soak up the atmosphere.

2. Tell the Manager of the Rink, or a friend who is a knowledgeable player, that you wish to become a curler. He will welcome you as a new recruit and will probably introduce you to the Ice Master or senior Ice-man who are experienced curling tutors. A solid grounding in the mechanics of the delivery of a stone is essential and the intelligent initiate will go to an expert to be taught this and to learn the rudiments of the game. There are far too many 'contortionist' curlers who cannot rid themselves of bad styles and habits evolved unaided in their early games.

3. It may be difficult to arrange lessons in the late afternoon or evening, when the ice is crowded, and you will probably be launched on your curling career in the morning, during the lunch period or at odd hours between curling sessions.

4. The Ice-man will advise you, to begin with, to play in shoes which will give you a reasonable grip on the ice as stability and balance are vital in the initial stages; a sliding sole on the left foot can come later. A heavy fall on slippery shoes will destroy confidence and make you wary of lifting the stone sufficiently and completing a full follow-through. The first aim is a simple, straightforward 'throw' while maintaining balance.

5. Do not despair when your first stones rumble forward a few yards – in the wrong direction – or cause alarm and raised eyebrows in the next rink. A beginner often finds that, instead of throwing the stone, the stone is throwing him. The Managers, Ice-Masters and Ice-men in Scotland are long-suffering men. They have seen it all before and will encourage you with remarks like: 'Try again, you'll soon improve.' They are right, of course, and it is a consolation to know that you cannot get worse!

6. In your series of lessons, you should be told to concentrate exclusively on draw weight. This means that you should try to draw stone after stone into the circles at the other end of the rink, and that you should not try to use heavier weight to hit other stones. The temptation to hit is strong, especially among school-boys, but it should be resisted. All early efforts should be directed towards the draw, and the 'touch' required for it, because at all levels – from club to world championship play – the draw is the shot that matters most, the basic shot in curling.

7. When your lessons end, it is time to practise, on your own or with a friend. For an hour over lunch-time almost every Saturday in the Edinburgh Ice Rink last season, a young girl practised to perfect an already excellent style of delivery. It is an example to be followed.

8. As you practise, you will meet other enthusiasts and this is the time to become a proficient sweeper. Help your friends by sweeping their stones and help yourself by co-ordinating the action of your broom with the movement of your feet. You will now also enlarge your repertoire of shots – by guarding, wick-ing, drawing through a port, raising and striking, – to end, per-haps, with the final flourish of a double take-out or the satisfac-tion of a cold draw round guards to the tee.

9. You are now ready to join a Club and play organised games. There are more than 600 registered Clubs in Britain, the vast majority of them in Scotland, and many Clubs in your area will welcome you. You will be placed in a rink for league play throughout the season and you will probably play lead, or the first stones in your rink. It is a wonderful position. Many top-class players make it their own and become specialist lead players. Respected Scottish skips will tell you that they played lead for the first five, eight or ten years of their curling careers. Now your hours of practice will pay dividends and you will be able to show your new club-mates how the first stones at each end should be played !

10. The final point – so important that we have placed it as a climax at the end of this ten-point plan – concerns curling courtesy. This is a vexed problem because, primarily, it is not the

beginner's responsibility but the responsibility of Club Office-bearers and skips to advise and guide new curlers along the proper lines, and, in too many cases, Clubs do not fulfil their obligations.

THE CURLING COURTESIES :

In addition to the Rules of Curling, to which we will graduate in a later chapter, there are unwritten laws which curlers obey as if they were in the Rule Book. These are the curling courtesies, or, in simple terms, the good manners of the ice. Properly observed, they bring order, dignity and feelings of well-being. Properly observe, therefore, the following customs :

Do not move when a player is about to deliver his stone. When waiting behind the hack to play, do not talk or stand close to your opponent when he is about to play – and keep clear of your opponents when they are sweeping. Equally, a skip should stand still behind the rings when his opposing skip is directing. (In Canada, it is normal for skips to stand directly behind the rings – to watch the complete course of the opposing stone – while, in Scotland, skips generally stand to a side.) The important thing is to stand still.

When the skip or acting skip is directing, do not crowd round the 'house' but take your place along the side of the rink and be ready to sweep the next stone for your side. Sweepers should never have to rush back to the hog to sweep; they should be already waiting there.

Never cross the middle of the ice when a player is on the hack ready to play.

The second player should keep an accurate record of the score after each end and adjust the scoreboard accordingly. This prevents any possibility of later confusion and an up-to-the-minute scoreboard is a courtesy to spectators.

Arrive on time on the ice, and, during the game, be ready to play when your turn comes. Waste of time, one of the bugbears of the game, sets the nerves of both sides on edge.

If the luck runs against you, keep cool. If you have a temper, control it. Because of the variation in ice surfaces, the expression,

'Take the rough with the smooth,' is well understood by curlers.

When a member of your side is off form, encourage him and humour him – a humorist is a decided asset on any rink. Curling is essentially a team game, so strive to foster team spirit.

Be quick to compliment a good shot – from either side – and never pass adverse comments or smile at an opponent's misfortune.*

Finally, we have an old curling saying in Scotland – 'the one thing you must do is to do what you're told'. Curlers who think that their skip is giving wrong directions should follow the wise advice given by J. D. Flavelle of Lindsay, Ontario, in 1896 : 'Speak to your skip quietly between the heads, suggesting where you think he is in error. If you fail to convince him, waive your judgment and carry out his instructions to the best of your ability.' A practice adopted by some curlers – to play for the skip's right or left leg instead of his broom – is not recommended. Far better to have a private word with the skip than to take your own ice. The simple rule is : obey your skip at all times, even when you think he is wrong.

---

* A Regulation framed by the Peebles Club in 1821 still applies: 'When a member falls and is hurt, the rest shall not laugh but render him every assistance to enable him to regain his former erect position.'

CHAPTER ELEVEN

THE DELIVERY

Let us now consider the method of *throwing* a stone – for you must throw it and not slide it or push it. This is the first law of the delivery.

The Rev. John Kerr wrote: 'The swing is to convey life to the stone and the eye must communicate the information by which the mind of the player determines what kind of life is needed. The hand is worked by the head and the head by the eye.' This is the second delivery law: Keep your head up and your eye on the skip's broom and never look down at the ice, or, as some players do, pick a line or patch on the ice to aim at.

With these two basic laws uppermost in your mind, you are now ready to take the first steps of your curling career, so let us proceed to the hack:

1. Place the ball of your right foot (or left foot if you are left-handed) firmly on the hack with the toe pointing up the ice to the far tee. The object is to keep your body in a square position facing the broom – at right angles to the direction of the stone. If your foot is placed at a side angle on the hack, there is a tendency for your body to shift from a square to a sideways position.

2. Sit down on the hack. Do not crouch over it but get down close to the ice with your left foot slightly ahead of you in a comfortable position – with the left toe, like the right toe, facing towards the far tee.

3. Hold your broom in the left hand. There are different ways of doing this. Some curlers hold the broom, balanced, in the middle and keep it at arm's length, using a high left-handed

action during the delivery. Some tuck the broom under the left
arm with the brush on the ice beside the left foot. It is a matter
of personal preference. But we advise you not to hold the end of
the handle with the brush on the ice at right angles to the direction of play, and we come down firmly against the practice of
discarding the broom before delivery because the broom balances
you on the left side against the weight of the stone on the right
side.

4. Clean the underside of the stone with your broom then
take hold of the handle of the stone again, with the fingers
underneath and the thumb on top – not with the full hand.
Great attention must be paid to the grip which should be firm
but light; under no circumstances should the handle be gripped
tightly with the full palm. To beginners, the instruction, 'firm
but light,' may seem a contradiction in terms. But it will soon
become apparent that a fierce grip not only results in a wristy
turn of the stone on delivery but also destroys the delicacy of
touch without which no curler can become a good curler.

5. You are now sitting comfortably on the hack with your
body square to the line of delivery, your head up, your eyes on
the broom at the other end of the ice, your feet both pointing
directly up the rink, your left hand holding your broom and
your right hand lightly holding the handle of the stone. Now
concentrate all your efforts on watching the broom at the far
end of the ice – or a mark on the barricade if no one is available to hold the broom during practice – and keep your head
as low as possible, to line up your shot, while your right arm
holds the stone on the ice as far ahead of you as possible. You
can now begin the delivery of the stone.

6. The secret of consistent accuracy in curling is to continue
to do the same thing time after time, in practice and under
stress in big games. It is exactly the same in golf, where the aim
is to achieve a grooved swing and keep it in the groove whatever
the state of the game. The best way to achieve this is to strive
for a classical swing, which is the simplest possible rhythmical
swing without embellishments, and, in curling, this must be to
lift the stone straight backwards and swing it straight forward

in a fluid pendulum movement. 'Straight back and straight forward' is the watchword of the delivery action.

7. Beginners are naturally anxious to retain their balance and a high back-swing is not advised in the early stages. To begin with, draw the stone back, lifting it only an inch or two on the back-swing, then return it to its forward position without throwing it. Do this again and again, lifting the stone a little higher each time at the full extent of the back-swing, before eventually throwing it. Later, you will lift the stone higher for a harder shot, but, for the moment, start with a modified back-swing. Remember, however, from your first attempt onwards, always lift the stone.

8. As you draw the stone back and lift it, you must straighten your right leg and raise your body, placing all your weight on your right foot on the hack. As you do this, you will find it necessary to counteract the weight of the stone on your right side and the best method of achieving this is to use the broom in your left hand as a balancing agent, and, at the same time, swing the left leg sideways.* This movement of the left leg takes various forms, the most extreme being an exaggerated sweep or kick, but the ideal form is a gentle sideways motion in unison with the back-swing of the stone. (Many first-class curlers keep the left foot stationary on the back-swing and some move it only an inch or two but we are convinced that the best type of delivery to teach a new curler involves a sideways movement of the left leg.)

9. You have now reached a position at the top of the back-swing – with the stone lifted off the ice behind your body, with all your weight on the right foot, with your left leg swung sideways and with your left arm, holding the broom, extended to the left. The forward motion begins with the body moving almost imperceptibly before the stone. This is in the nature of things and should not be considered by the beginner but it is of vital importance that the body should be *behind* the stone at the point of delivery.

* Many Canadians now swing the left foot backwards rather than to the side.

10. As the forward motion gains momentum, your weight shifts from the right foot to the left foot, which slides forward on the ice as you *sole* the stone.

11. Proper soling of the stone is vital for a successful shot and can only come with practice. It means that the stone is not dropped or banged down on the ice but that it is thrown smoothly and without any rocking movement. Bad soling spreads unhappiness all round; if the stone is bumped on delivery, the player is unhappy with his shot and the other seven players are unhappy with the hole he has left in the ice !

12. As the stone reaches the ice, the left foot slides forward with it, while the right foot, its work done, drags along the ice behind the body.

13. You throw the stone directly it is soled on the ice – we will deal later with the sliding delivery – and, as you do so, your right arm swings forward in a full follow-through directed at the skip's broom. The follow-through, which should be fully completed before raising the body from the ice, is often neglected by curlers who complete the other movements admirably but spoil their performance with a poor last act.

14. We have left to the last the all-important question of imparting the in-turn or the out-turn to the stone – to make it curve to the right or left – and have done so advisedly because, with so many other things to think about, it is well to develop this art at a later stage. A special heading is required for the 'turn', which is little understood by a large section of the curling community and even by many competent curlers.

THE 'TURN' :

The old expressions, 'elbow in' and 'elbow out', are the most misguided terms that could have been used to describe the turn of a stone. Bent arms may have been common in the old days but elbows should not be mentioned in the same breath as the delivery of a curling stone for the arm should be swung from the shoulder and the elbow should not be bent.

The far more accurate 'in-hand' and 'out-hand' or 'in-turn' and 'out-turn', are activated in different ways. We believe that, at the start of the delivery, the handle of the stone should be pointing up and down the rink, and that, when the stone is soled, the handle should be in the same position. But there are no hard and fast rules on this and top-class curlers set the handle at various angles for delivery.

The important feature is that the 'handle' or 'turn' should be given to the stone at the very last moment before the handle is released and that this movement should eventually be so natural that it becomes part of the subconscious. In other words, the turn to be played will be noted when sizing up a shot before delivery and not consciously considered during delivery.

Constant practice will make perfect this 'turn' technique, and, in addition, will impart to the stone the *amount* of turn which will bring the greatest control to the shot. For example, the handle of the stone should make three to three and a quarter complete turns between delivery and the far tee to give maximum draw with a drawing shot. (This applies to stones delivered direct from the hack, not stones released further up the ice by long-sliders.)

It is well known that a 'birling' stone – that is, a stone which is rotating quickly or spinning – does not draw nearly so much as a stone with the correct amount of handle. Again, a stone with too little turn imparted to it tends to lose its handle, or change its handle, and consequently, the shot is missed. This happens frequently with beginners and occasionally with all curlers and is a humbling experience, especially if the stone has left the hand on target!

On outdoor ice, with its rougher patches and bumps, more handle is often required to keep a stone on its proper course and the experienced curler will adjust accordingly.

One last observation on the 'turn'. Because it is generally supposed that the in-turn or in-hand shot is the easier to play, it is assumed to be the natural turn. It is true that almost all beginners are taught first to play the in-turn and the vast majority of skips start an end by directing their leads to play in-turn shots. But here, despite writings and arguments to the contrary, we accept the ruling of old-time Scottish curlers that the natural hand is the out-hand. In former times, Scots skips meant the out-hand when they shouted to team-mates to play the 'natural hand'. When first studying this contradictory evidence, we handed miniature curling stones to our two sons, then aged about ten and eight, and asked them to throw the stones along the drawing-room carpet to circles marked in chalk at the far end of the room. Knowing nothing about curling, nothing about stones and certainly nothing about 'turns', both boys threw out-hand shots.

We must complete this section on the delivery of a curling stone with a personal conviction which lies near to our heart. Whatever styles have been suggested, whatever shoulds and should-nots have been stated, it remains true that almost all games-players have their individual idiosyncrasies, little quirks of style all their own which, in the case of better-known players, become their trademarks.

Many first-class curlers place the right foot at a sharp angle on the hack or perform an elephant-like shuffle with the left foot on the back-swing; many lift the stone almost head-high to show, in the words of the old saying, the bottom of the stone to the sun, while some 'ride' the stone or push it; many add extra movements for which there appears to be no point except to satisfy the players themselves.

We offer guide-lines towards the ideal type of delivery but do not expect them to be followed in every aspect. There are very few curlers with deliveries we can call classical. All the others vary one or other of the movements to some extent and the player with a real talent, even genius, for the game may vary more than the others.

But all good curlers, including those with that little extra who play in the rarified atmosphere at the pinnacle of the game, have attained their position with styles which are soundly based on the first principles of the delivery. Beginners should bear this in mind in their early struggles with stones.

CHAPTER TWELVE

THE SLIDING DELIVERY AND
TAKE-OUT TECHNIQUE

THE DELIVERY CALLED the 'Slide' or the 'Long Slide' was introduced by Canadian curlers. Ken Watson, famous skip who won the last of his three Canadian Championships in 1949, has been called the first long-slider and there is no doubt that his successes inspired many young curlers to follow his example. But Ken writes that, in his best and most supple years, he released the handle of the stone no more than a foot or two beyond the centre of the rings although his slide took him half-way between the front rings and the hog score.

What is certain is that the 'Slide' brought youngsters into the game in Canada in their thousands. Attracted by the spectacular grace of a balanced long slide, young Canadians developed more and more leg thrust from the secure Canadian hacks, and, with sliding soles on their shoes, vied with each other for length of slide. In their competitive enthusiasm, many of them concentrated more on the slide than on the quality of their play.

The game in Canada became clouded in an air of unreality as the young men tilted at the 'establishment' and hit the headlines. Games of curling became acrobatic circus acts and the final comedy was eventually staged in February, 1955, at the Town of Mount Royal Curling Club in Montreal, when, in an exhibition game, Stan Austman of Saskatoon, third player in Saskatchewan's school championship rink, astounded the gallery by sliding the whole length of the rink to deposit his stone on the tee while still retaining enough momentum to slide on through the house!

The Canadian legislators, who had previously defended the long slide because it had brought so many schoolboys into the game, were forced to act, and, a month later, the wording, 'and the player shall not slide beyond the hog-line nearest the hack from which the stone has been delivered' was introduced to the Rule Book. The Rule has since been altered slightly and standardised (See Royal Club Rule 58 in a later chapter).

The 'Slide', which is used in varying degrees by thousands of Canadian and American rinks, by many Scots who aspire to top-class competition and increasingly in other European countries, should be approached with caution. Arthur Frame, the indefatigable Secretary of the Glasgow Province, who, it is said, reads the *Annuals* of the Royal Club when he cannot sleep at nights, made a telling point when he wrote : 'some of the young curlers deliver a stone and find themselves on the middle of a sheet of ice, looking rather like a stork who has missed his breakfast fish !'

We have seen inefficient sliders finishing in an undignified sprawl facing the next rink and even facing the hack they have just left while their stones near the house at the far end – probably on the wrong course. Such curlers should cut down on their slide and aim for balance and control.

The long-sliding delivery starts in the same way as the normal delivery, but, on the forward swing, the player thrusts much more strongly from the hack with his right leg and slides far out on the ice with a slippery sole on his left shoe. The slippery sole can be leather or some synthetic material which is cut from a sheet and attached to the shoe. In some cases, sliding pads are supplied with curling shoes or boots.

The delivery is not for beginners or average players or for those in middle age or over. Other governing factors are an athletic build and a desire to play a take-out game. Of itself, a long slide is not the passport to a higher class of curling. There are many thousands of expert curlers who use a standing delivery (with no slide), or a modified slide, and the main reasons why the top players in the world's most competitive events are long-sliders are that they are young, athletic men with the keen eyes of youth – these two factors being far more important than the 'Slide'.

When playing running shots (fast stones), long-sliders release the stone at roughly the same position as other curlers. But, when drawing or guarding, they keep hold of the handle until well past the centre of the rings and often until a point near the hog score, and keep their heads down behind the stone until the release of the handle. This graceful movement presents problems, such as riding the stone, loss of timing in delivery, pushing the stone off with a wristy action when imparting the turn and loss of balance or direction – the riding of the stone (with the stone under the curler instead of in front of him) and the final push being the most common long-sliding faults. Only curlers of considerable skill can overcome these difficulties and beginners are earnestly advised to strive for a modified slide at most – at least until they take their bearings on the unknown ice!

The long-sliding delivery, and the wide-open take-out type of game which goes with it, were brought to Scotland by the Richardson family rink – Ernie Richardson (skip), Arnold Richardson (third player), Garnet Richardson (second player) and Wes Richardson (lead). Ernie has skipped his rink to a record four wins in the Canadian Championships and four wins in the World Championship for the Scotch Whisky Cup,* a performance which has rightly earned for the Richardsons a place among the immortals of the game.

The clear-cut victories of this famous Canadian rink over Scottish teams in the early Scotch Whisky Cup games, from 1959 to 1963, sent Scots curlers home in pensive mood. The new take-out technique, played by curlers of the calibre of the Richardsons, seemed unbeatable. Strong criticisms were voiced, particularly (a) that long-sliders gained an unfair advantage by sliding yards up the ice before delivery, and (b) that they delivered in the position, with the head directly behind the stone, of a billiard player and could thus adjust the direction of slow shots while sliding. The long-sliders made the counter-claim that they committed themselves to the shot with their action while

* The World Championship Trophy is now the Air Canada Silver Broom.

still in the hack and that any attempted adjustment while sliding would hinder rather than help the shot.

Whatever the secret weapon, there is an answer to it. It soon became obvious to students of the game in Scotland that the answer to the take-out game, when played by top-class Canadians, was – the take-out game. Attempts to draw to the face of opposing stones was not practical; no players in the world could be expected to 'freeze'* consistently against stones, and, if the attempted 'freezes' were an inch or two short or strong, narrow or wide, the next strike by opponents as accurate as the Richardsons destroyed the tactic. As the strike, on the other hand, was the easiest shot in curling, the answer, undoubtedly, was to play the Canadians at their own game.

The first Scottish rink to make a positive effort to adopt the new technique was Chuck Hay and his team. Chuck, who has acknowledged his debt to Ernie Richardson for help and encouragement, realised that the Canadian wide-open game was the winning game. How well he and his team applied themselves to learn the new type of play can be gauged by the rink's wonderfully consistent record in World Championship play, culminating in their dramatic victory in the event in 1967. The winning rink in that year was Chuck Hay, John Bryden, Alan Glen and David Howie – all Perthshire farmers,

The take-out game sets a premium on accuracy, fitness and nerve because one miss can be more costly than in other types of play. When rinks are down, they lay stones short of the rings, and, if they are missed by attempted opposition strikes, the losing rinks then draw behind the front stones to gain shots. But the basic plan – and, of course, there are many variations – is as follows:

Team A draws to the side of the house. Team B strikes out

---

* The freeze shot, acknowledged to be the most difficult shot in the game, is to draw a stone alongside another stone and directly in front of it, without touching it or only just touching it. When played perfectly, the stone cannot be removed by a strike because it is completely checked by the other stone. The old Scottish instruction for the shot is 'crack an egg on it'.

A further variety of delivery styles are shown by Alex Torrance and his rink. *From top:* Alex F. Torrance, Alex Torrance, Bobby Kirkland and Jimmy Waddell

From Left : Chuck Hay directs an in-hand shot, the stone being aimed at the broom to curl in to the stone on the tee; John Bryden directs his player to throw an out-hand shot to nudge back an opposing stone on the tee; Alex F. Torrance gives the signal to guard his winner; and Alex Torrance calls for a full strike to drive the front stone to the back stones to clear the 'house'. *Below :* The Torrance rink show the power of their sweeping, all four members of the rink combining to coax the stone forward

the stone and lies shot. Team A follows with a similar shot and so on until the Skip counts one shot with the last stone.

However accurate the players, this sequence occurs very rarely. A player will strike out the shot and his own stone will also roll out, leaving an empty house. The next player will then draw, starting the routine as before.

But, if Team A lays a stone on the left of the house and Team B misses it, Team A then lays the next stone on the right of the house – square with the first stone to eliminate the possibility of a double take-out by the opposition – and Team A then lies two shots and Team B is in trouble. But, if Team B removes one of Team A's stones and the B stone stays in the house, and Team A misses that stone, Team B has only to take out the other Team A stone to lie two shots.

Such a quick change of fortune underlines the vital importance of each stone played. The resultant strain imposed on all members of a rink is the special feature of the take-out game. As the last stone is vitally important, the skips bear a further strain as they jostle for position towards the end of a close game, and, with their last stone at a late stage, they may try to 'blank' an end (leave nothing in the house) in order to retain the last stone at the next end.

Another feature is bare houses* with few stones in play, which reduces the possibility of lucky rubs and wicks to a minimum. This is a source of further controversy among Scots who have been bred on the traditional type of draw game which includes all the shots. ('Apartments to Let' was the term once used to describe an empty house.) The argument against the take-out game is that, on good ice, the players concentrate on two shots, the strike and the draw, and the many 'kittle' or delicate shots – like the angled guard, the six-foot raise to the tee, the wick past other stones, the draw through a port or even a double port

---

* 'When the order of the day is "Strike, strike", bare rink-heads are the consequence and no opportunity presents for wicking, cannoning, drawing, porting and guarding, which bring out the science of the combatants and constitute that beauty and fascination in the spiel which alike invigorates the body and braces the mind.' From *Memorabilia Curliana Mabenensia,* by Sir Richard Broun, Bt. 1830.

– are lost to the game; and that, because of this, the whole character of the game is changing for the worse.

On bad ice, or ice affected by weather, Television lights or crowds, it is not possible to achieve the accuracy needed for the straight take-out game, and, on such occasions, curlers are forced to play a greater variety of shots. In this connection, we believe that bad ice is no bad thing for a major competition. It separates the men from the boys, and, while giving all curlers the opportunity to use their brains, gives the top-quality striking rinks – as against the strikers who cannot adapt when the ice beats them – the chance to prove that they can win on any ice. Good 'strikers' in top-class rinks, of course, are also masters of the basic draw shot, and, in addition, many of them use little more than hack-weight for take-out shots.

A positive argument against the draw game is that its exponents tend to become obsessed with draw weight. The extreme case is expressed in the claim : 'Did you see that great end with all sixteen stones in the house?' The ignorance of such a remark is exposed when it is shown how many striking chances were missed. Without doubt, an aggressive draw game is the only successful type of draw game.

An unattractive facet of the striking game is the 'tactical' stone which is deliberately thrown through the house to leave the opposition nothing to work on. There are faults on both sides but there is no doubt that the take-out game is the winning game at the highest level.

To sum up, the take-out school aim to simplify the game, to cut the number of stones in play to a minimum – to reduce the chances of lucky shots – to place a greater premium of accuracy on all shots played, and, consequently, to set all players a more challenging test of nerve and skill. The supporters of the aggressive draw game aim to build 'heads' of stones, to play all the shots known in curling, and thus enjoy a greater variety of satisfying situations, and to accept the 'rubs' for or against as part of the game.

Many curlers claim that the draw game is far more interesting to watch and that the take-out game, with its concentration on strike and draw to the virtual exclusion of all else, is poor value for the spectators. This point, of course, is irrelevant when you consider that curling has always been a participation sport. Certainly the draw game, with more stones in play, presents a greater general interest to spectators, but, while a series of misses can make the take-out game deadly dull, it can promote high excitement in the galleries if the two rinks hit form together and feelings of suspense are built up as the audience waits for the misses which count.

The controversy continues and it is good for the game. Curling has become a young man's game at the top and this is also good for the game. Possibly five per cent of the world population of curlers play take-out and the rest play a draw, aggressive draw or modified take-out game; and, remember, the long-sliders, who now dominate the highly-competitive scene, will become short-sliders as they grow older.

There are good and bad players of all types and the sensible approach to 'draw' and 'take-out' is that there is room for both in a game in which crack players and rank bad players equally enjoy themselves within the brotherhood of the broom.

CHAPTER THIRTEEN

THE ART OF SWEEPING

'Soop, lads, so-o-op!'

CURLING HAS BEEN described as 'bowls on ice', We prefer the description of bowls as 'curling on grass', but, however you judge the two games, the comparison between them is valid. The number of players per side, the rotation of play and the scoring system are the same. Bowls take 'bias', stones take 'the hand' and skips direct team members to play roughly similar shots although striking is less certain at bowls because of the elliptical shape of 'woods'.

But there are two major differences in play. The first, and less important, is that, while early bowls at an end are generally played behind the jack, which may be struck towards them, stones are more valuable if they are short of the centre of the circles and 'in the way of promotion' to the tee. The second, and all-important, difference is that, because of sweeping, all four players in a rink take an active part in every stone played – the skip skipping, the player playing and the two sweepers sweeping.

We look back with awe to the hardy Ayrshire curlers 150 years ago who played on the lochs in their stocking soles, and, when short of besoms, plied the ice with their Kilmarnock bonnets. Today's equipment is infinitely more efficient than a bonnet, and, with the modern tools, it is the workman who is at fault if his sweeping is ineffective.

Good sweeping, satisfying to the curler and a delight to watch, adds greatly to a player's stature and is a match-winning factor. The recipe is simple for it is much easier to be a first-class sweeper than a first-class curler. The main ingredients are power and rhythm.

But, first, let us dispose of the argument which crops up periodically, even in the best-informed cirles, that sweeping is so much wasted effort. It is true that on wet ice or ice heavy with hoar frost, sweeping has little or no effect. But mechanical tests in Switzerland in 1924, and later tests in Canada,* while proving inconclusive on certain types of ice, provided statistical evidence that, on good clean ice, a well-swept stone will travel twelve feet or more further than an unswept stone.

In addition, sweeping reduces the amount of draw of a stone, keeping the stone on a straighter course, so that the sweepers can bring a stone past a guard and make all the difference between a hit and a miss.

The technical reasons for sweeping are threefold:

1. To brush any dust or impurities from the path of the stone.

2. To reduce the atmospheric pressure in front of the stone and to create a minor vacuum which draws the stone on. (It is essential, therefore, to sweep as close to the stone as possible.)

3. To cause a temporary melting of the ice producing a water lubrication and consequent low friction at the leading portion of the stone.

Numbers 2 and 3 emphasise the need for power in sweeping. The broom is not for leaning on and it is no use whatever rubbing lightly or tickling the surface of the ice. Good sweepers should feel their muscles tingling after a game; in boxing parlance, they should know they have been in a fight.

Rhythmical sweeping means that leg and body movements should be allied to the action of the arms and that the co-ordinated effort should be maintained throughout a game and used at all but the fastest speeds of a running stone. A rhythmical sweeping action, of course, is far less tiring than jerking movements or leg actions which make it awkward for a curler to keep pace with a faster stone.

* Stones were swung and thrown from a tripod by means of a trigger mechanism.

In Scotland, the two sweepers work on either side of the stone and as close together as possible while both sweepers in top Canadian rinks operate on one side. Sweeping with the Canadian corn broom is more spectacular than sweeping with Scottish brushes and sweepers of the calibre of Bernie Sparkes and Fred Storey of the Ron Northcott rink (three times Canadian and World Champions) are a joy to watch as they pound the ice in perfect unison.*

Less attractive as a spectacle, Scottish sweeping is more economical in style, less wasteful of effort, and, for this reason, we believe that the Scots brush is more effective than the Canadian broom, which flaps in the air to the left and right between strokes while all the effort of brush strokes is concentrated on the spot which matters – on the ice directly in front of the stone.

Those who have watched the well-known Torrance rink from the Hamilton and Thornyhill Club will appreciate what strong sweeping can do to a laggard stone. All members of the rink are expert sweepers and sometimes all four of them will labour together to achieve that little extra which means so much. For example, when third player Alex Torrance throws a stone which needs to be swept, he quickly joins Bobby Kirkland and Jimmy Waddell, and, as the stone nears the house, skip Alex F. Torrance rushes out to add his weight to a combined effort which coaxes the stone to give a vital extra turn before it dies. (The practice of skips joining their sweepers is not recommended except in cases where nothing is to be gained by watching the direction of the stone from the house.)

* In his *History of the Sanquhar Curling Society* (1874), James Brown gives us a graphic description of 'tall, strapping young men' at Wanlockhead, whose sweeping discipline was 'absolutely perfect' at the time when there were eight players in a rink: 'Arranged three and three on each side of the rink, they waited with the greatest attention till the stone was delivered, followed it quietly but eagerly in its course, till, at the call of the skip, "soop her up", down came the besoms like lightning, hands were clasped, the feet kept time to the rapid strokes of the besom and no exertion was spared until the stone was landed at the desired spot, when, a good long breath being drawn, the player was rewarded with a universal shout, "weel played, mon!" '

Always sweep at right angles to the direction of the stone, not at an angle, and in front, not to the side, of a stone. This is common sense but a study of sweepers will show that this sense is not so common! Be careful also not to touch the stone, but, if you do, immediately declare the fact that you have 'burnt the stone'* and remove it from play. This is a Rule but it is the sporting instinct of a curler more than the written word which prompts him to act, even if his broom has only just touched the stone and has not appeared to affect the course of the stone in any way.

One final point which should prove helpful to apprentice sweepers. Beginners will find that some of their fellow curlers prefer to sweep on one side rather than the other. The simple solution to a possible clash of interests between 'one-sided' curlers is to practise sweeping to the left and right so that you become equally proficient on either side.

'It is the broom that wins the battle,' wrote the Rev. John Kerr, and no experienced sweeper needs proof of this 'sweeping statement'. A good sweeper does not need tests to convince him of the value of his efforts. He already *knows* because he can *see* the stone surging forward and *feel* its added impetus behind his broom.

---

* 'To burn: one is said to be burnt when he has suffered in any attempt. Ill burnt: having suffered severely. To derange any part of a game by improper interference, as in curling, to burn a stane.' Excerpt from Jamieson's *Scottish Dictionary*.

CHAPTER FOURTEEN

CURLING DRESS

FIFTEEN YEARS AGO, we were asked by a Canadian curler for a
report on the curling dress in general use in Scotland.* The
answer, devastating to the clothes-conscious Canadian, was like
a naval signal, brief and to the point : 'There is no curling dress
in Scotland.'

At that time, Scotsmen curled in their business suits, farm
clothes or sports jackets. Some took off their jackets
and curled in their waistcoats while others played with light
cardigans in conservative colours, usually grey or lovat green,
over their waistcoats. Knickerbockers and the less attractive
baggy plus-fours used by golfers were in evidence. The starched
white collars of the business world were common on the rink,
and, for a spell midway between the two Great Wars, one rink
wore hard 'pot hats', a distinctive if severe uniform which
prompted an opposition skip to remark, after a heavy defeat,
that he had just attended his own funeral !

A number of curlers actually wore special jerseys but a jersey
with a club badge was a talking point and four men in the same
uniform stopped the game on adjoining rinks.

Historical references are more exciting. The Minutes of the
Rosslyn Club report that, 120 years ago, the mother
of Colonel Wedderburn knitted worsted vests and presented
them to the members of the five rinks in the Club. In the same

* For many years before this, Canadian curlers dressed as rinks and
the Canadian Championship was, and is, a blaze of colour with the rinks
representing all the Provinces dressed in their own sweaters and crests.
Canadians and Americans were talking of well-dressed curlers when
Scots were taking off their jackets and draping them over the barricade
at the end of the ice before a game.

96

Above: Ernie Richardson's renowned rink from Saskatchewan who hold the record number of wins in the Canadian Championship and the World Championship (four in each). *From Left:* Wes Richardson, Garnet Richardson, Arnold Richardson and Ernie Richardson (Skip). Mel Perry was lead in the last of these four wins – in 1963. *Below:* A typical example of a long-sliding Canadian delivery, illustrated by Ron Northcott, who, with three World and Canadian successes to his credit, now rivals Ernie Richardson as one of the greatest skips in Canadian history

Picture of power. An immensely strong sweeper, George Fink (third player in Ron Northcott's World Championship rink in 1966) shows how to wield a Canadian broom

period, the Abdie Club decreed that every member, except the Chaplain, must wear the club uniform – a blue coat with sixteen large buttons and a buff vest with eight small buttons, each button engraved with the club crest. In 1850, the Royal Club itself proposed a uniform for curlers initiated at Curlers' Courts, the uniform to be 'coat, vest and trousers of one pattern and quality, the groundwork of the cloth to be as nearly as possible of a granite colour, checked with blue and green bars, the blue being the royal colour and the green emblematic of the broom'. The material was to cost 4s. 6d. per yard and the cost of making the uniform 32s. but trade was poor for John Piper, the Royal Club's official clothier, and this granite, blue and green creation is, mercifully, heard of no more.

At the turn of the century, Members of the Pitlochry Club were obliged to wear Atholl tartan trousers, red waistcoats with brass buttons, double-breasted blue reefer jackets with buttons, on which the motif was a curling stone, and balmorals. The Breadalbane Aberfeldy Club members wore Breadalbane tartan trousers, red vests, blue coats with Breadalbane buttons and blue balmorals edged with tartan.

There were many other club uniforms in the days when curling was exclusively an outdoor sport, the most famous being the dress worn by members of the Dunkeld Club, whose present Secretary, Tom P. Stewart, is the 1969–70 President of the Royal Club. The dress – Atholl tartan trews, blue waistcoat with red piping, blue jacket with red collar and red cuffs and the Atholl bonnet which is the same as that worn by the Scottish Horse – has added colour to many Grand Matches and is still used by a number of members on these occasions and at Club dinners. The bonnet was designed by the Atholl family and the late Duke of Atholl, the founder and Commanding Officer of the Scottish Horse, adopted the bonnet for use by the Dunkeld Club, of which the present Duke of Atholl is President.

Club uniforms faded from the scene with the spread of indoor Ice Rinks and a survey in 1954 revealed that only a few Clubs had their own dress, among them the Gangrels Club in Ayrshire and the Glendoick Club in Perthshire, the members of which

D

created a new badge for the 1950 Canadian Tour in Scotland. Two famous skips, John Robertson of Glasgow and Alex Mayes of Falkirk, took the ice with rinks wearing jerseys of the same colour. In Glasgow, the Crossmyloof Club* had a cloth badge and the Carmunnock and Rutherglen Club had just designed one.

The 1954 survey, published in *The Scottish Curler* magazine, was quickly followed by a circular from the Royal Club announcing that 'a measure of uniformity in dress' had been agreed for the Royal Club tour in the United States in January, 1955.

The twenty Scots who made that first Scottish Tour in U.S.A. wore dark blue blazers, and, for curling, light blue sweaters with crests. Mrs Horace Vaile, Chicago, who met the team as she was leaving to be joint-captain of the first group of Canadian and American ladies to tour in Scotland, said, on arrival at Prestwick: 'The Scots, in their smart uniforms, were wonderful and made our lady curlers swoon.' Having waved bon voyage to the twenty Scotsmen only a few days before, we told Mrs Vaile that she must have been watching a different team!

The year 1955 was the turning point. From this time on, 'curlers' claes'† changed out of all recognition in Scottish Ice Rinks. Dozens of clubs prepared cloth badges to sew on club jerseys. Jimmy Neilson of the Dippool Club and his highly-successful rink were among the leaders with yellow jerseys and other top-class rinks followed their lead. A Royal Club tie, designed by Colonel William Drummond, was first seen in all the Rinks in 1955. The Glasgow Province tie, introduced two years before, was followed by other Provincial ties.

---

* An excerpt from the *Ordnance Gazetteer of Scotland*, edited by Francis H. Groome, is interesting. 'Crossmyloof: at a council of war here, according to a popular myth, Queen Mary, on the morning of the battle of Langside, laid a small crucifix on her hand, saying "as surely as that cross lies on my loof (hand), I will this day fight the Regent" – hence the name Crossmyloof'. The centrepiece of the Crossmyloof Curling Club badge is a cross on a hand.

† The words, 'Dress: Curlers' Claes', are traditionally inserted on tickets for curling suppers and functions in Scotland.

The ladies also adopted club colours to add to the tartan skirts which had been their standard dress. (Tartan skirts are still the general dress among Scots lady curlers; ski-type trousers are also used but are less popular).

And what of the kilt for men? In his book, *The Complete Curler* (1914), J. Gordon Grant said on the subject of clothes: 'Well, that is a matter of taste, and sometimes very bad taste at that. Possibly, for freedom of action, the kilt is the best curling dress extant.' We are not sure that Gordon Grant was right, nor are ninety-nine per cent of the curlers of Scotland.

In one important aspect of dress, Scots differ diametrically from Canadians, large numbers of whom, including many of their best players, wear gloves. Scots do not, believing that gloves affect the feel on the handle of a stone.

Today, Scottish curlers dress for the game and a large proportion of them play in club or Ice Rink jerseys. The change, which was long overdue, has brought colour to the game – to add to the red and blue circles on the ice which were introduced in Scottish Ice Rinks in recent years. Many curlers also feel that dressing the part helps their performance, and, when all four members of a rink are dressed the same, fosters team spirit.

As in every sport, the beginner should aim to be comfortably dressed. Clothes should fit and sweaters and cardigans should not be too heavy because new curlers, who will play lead or second, will constantly be called upon to sweep and sweeping is hot work; after a hard game, beginners will find aches in all sorts of new places.

One part of the anatomy is particularly important in any discussion on dress – the neck – and we will stick *our* neck out to say that curlers should wear a sports shirt without a tie, or, if a tie is worn, that it should be worn loosely. The eyes must be clear and relaxed when the curler goes down on the hack to play his stone – not bulging with the exertion of sweeping the last stone for his side with a tightly-knotted tie.

CHAPTER FIFTEEN

FOOTWEAR

FROM THE DAWN of the game, curling stones have been a curler's most prized possessions. Now that matched sets of stones have been introduced to the Ice Rinks and Scottish curlers do not use their own stones, the most important items of personal equipment are curling shoes or boots.

This is a purely personal choice for each curler but the footwear best suited to his needs should be 'evolved' after much thought. Beginners should experiment with different soles, and different soles on the left and right shoes, bearing in mind that, in the early stages, a left sole with too much slide will make a difficult series of movements even more difficult.

A recent development, the sliding left foot came into the Scottish game in step with the take-out technique. A few short years ago, Scottish Ice Rinks charged approximately a shilling to enter the Rink, four shillings for a three-hour curling session, one shilling to hire a pair of stones and sixpence to hire goloshes. Now, the charge for a two and a half-hour session is between eight and ten shillings and goloshes are not on offer – although helpful Ice Rink Managers and Ice-men will usually find a pair somewhere for the forgetful curler. (Curlers used to arrive early to search through the bundles of goloshes for good-fitting pairs and we remember one farmer, a giant of a man, who managed, after much heaving and grunting, to fit on the largest pair available – size 14!)

A curler wearing certain types of rubber soles will find that, when the ice is sticky, his left foot will grip and he will stumble awkwardly instead of sliding forward on delivery. This affects performance and destroys confidence. Some curlers change to another shoe in such a situation and others carry a sock in their pocket and slip it over the left shoe before playing a stone.

A few wear waterproof leggings to save wetting their knees as they slide; for the same reason, some Scots wear knee pads, which are in widespread use in Switzerland.

There are fifty-seven varieties of approach to curling footwear and leg-wear. Again, beginners should aim for simplicity – flannel trousers for the legs, and, for the early practice periods at least, rubber-soled shoes or boots, from which they can graduate, as they master the swing, to a more slippery sole on the left foot.

The object is to be able to curl with confidence, to play the game on a sensible footing!

CHAPTER SIXTEEN

THE RULES OF THE GAME

As we have indicated, the Rules of Curling have changed little since they were first introduced in Scotland in 1839. In the Royal Club's pocket-sized Constitution and Rules booklet, the actual rules of play take up only four pages.

While certain refinements have been made in recent years, the Rules Committees of the Royal Club are constantly on their guard against needless alterations and additions, however plausible the reasons for them may be, and almost all curlers are grateful that the rules of the game – only eighteen in number with a small additional section which applies to Royal Club Competitions – are short and uncomplicated. The minority who press for further legislation, stricter control and more penalties, either do not appreciate or care to disregard the three fundamental reasons for keeping the Rules as brief and simple as possible :

1. However many new Rules are introduced, and however carefully they are worded, there will always be loopholes or situations which are not covered. (The highly complex Rules of Golf, and the book of interpretations which go with them, do not cover all possible eventualities, and never will.)

2. Curlers, proud of their sporting reputation, are expected to interpret the Rules sportingly and experience has shown that this expectation has been amply fulfilled. In other words, curlers obey the spirit as well as the letter of the law, and, when situations occur which are not specifically covered in the Rules, the skips mutually agree on a course of action.

3. The general feeling among curlers is that any penalties incurred should be self-imposed. For example, if a curler touches a played stone belonging to his side, he himself will re-

move it from the ice. The Umpire is very rarely called in to settle disputes and generally acts only when measuring stones at the conclusion of ends. To increase the penalties in the Rule Book would eventually endanger that happy position.

W. J. (Bill) Mackay, President of the Canadian Branch of the Royal Club, found unanimous favour at the 1968 Royal Club Annual Meeting at Peebles when he said: 'I would like to throw the Rules out of the window. For a man to be a true curler is the important point. If he is, there is no need of Rules.'

While all curlers should know the Rules, and should constantly refer to them to refresh their knowledge, Bill Mackay's view is commonly held and it stresses the sensible sporting approach to a game which is not bedevilled by players who try to take an unfair advantage. The question, 'When is a curler not a curler?' is easily answered. 'When he intentionally breaks the Rules.'

We are delighted, therefore, to use so little space in this book with

THE RULES OF CURLING

(Note: Rules 1–42 cover the general regulations and conditions of the Royal Club.)

THE RINK

43. The length of the Rink from the Foot Score to the Tee shall, subject to the provisions of rules 45 and 64, be 42 yards.

44. The Tees shall be 38 yards apart – and, with the Tees as centres, Circles having a radius of 6 feet shall be drawn. Additional inner Circles may also be drawn.

45. In alignment with the Tees, lines, to be called Centre lines, may be drawn from the Tees to points 4 yards behind each Tee, and at these points Foot Scores, 18 inches in length, shall be drawn at right angles, on which, at 6 inches from the Centre line, the heel of the Hack shall be placed. When Hack and Crampit are both being used in the same Rink, the Crampit shall be placed immediately behind the Hack 6 inches from the Centre line.

46. Other Scores shall be drawn across the Rink at right angles to the Centre lines as in the Diagram, *viz.*:

(*a*) A 'Hog Score', distant from each Tee, one-sixth part of the distance between the 'Foot Score' and the farther Tee.

(*b*) A 'Sweeping Score', across each outer Circle and through each Tee.

(*c*) A 'Back Score', behind and just touching the outside of each outer Circle.

NOTE. – In forming Rinks the Diagram should be referred to.

THE RULES OF THE GAME :

47. All Curling-Stones shall be of a circular shape. No Stone, including handle and bolt, shall be of greater weight than 44 lbs. or of greater circumference than 36 inches, or of less height than one-eighth part of its greatest circumference.

48. No Stone shall be substituted for another (except under rule 49 or rule 59) after a Match has been begun, but the sole of a Stone may be reversed at any time during a Match, provided the player be ready to play when his turn comes.

49. Should a Stone be broken, the largest fragment shall be counted for that Head – the player being entitled to use another Stone, or another pair, during the remainder of the Match.

50. Any Stone which rolls over, or comes to rest on its side or top, shall be removed from the ice.

51. Should the handle quit the Stone in delivery, the player shall be entitled to replay the shot.

52. Every Stone which does not clear the Hog Score shall be a Hog, and must be removed from the ice, but no Stone shall be considered a Hog which has struck another Stone lying in position. A Stone passing the Back Score, and lying clear of it, must be removed from the ice, as also any Stone which in its progress touches swept snow on either side of the Rink or sides or divisions of Indoor Rinks.

53. All Matches shall be of a certain number of Heads, or Shots, or by Time as may be agreed on, or as fixed by the Umpire at the outset. In the event of Competitors' scores being equal, play may be continued for one or more Heads as may be agreed on, or as provided for by the conditions of the Match, or as may be fixed by the Umpire.

Diagram to be drawn on the Ice and referred to throughout the Rules as
'THE RINK'

SCALE OF FEET

────── COMPULSORY

---------- OPTIONAL

DIRECTIONS

1. The Tees shall be 38 yards apart.

2. Around each Tee draw a circle having a radius of 6 feet.

[Inner circles may also be drawn.]

3. In alignment with the Tees, centre lines may be drawn to points 4 yards behind each Tee.

4. Draw scores across the Rink at right angles to the central line, viz.:

(*a*) The *Foot Score* – 18 inches in length, 4 yards behind each Tee.

(*b*) The *Back Score* – behind and just touching the outside of each outer circle.

(*c*) The *Sweeping Score* – across each outer circle and through each Tee.

(*d*) The *Hog Score* – distant from the Tee one-sixth part of the distance between the Foot Score and the farther Tee.

When a Match is being played by time, no Head may be started excepting an extra or deciding Head after the time signal has been given. A Head shall be deemed to have started when the Skip is in position and the first player is on the Hack or Crampit ready to play his Stone.

54. Every Rink of players shall be composed of four-a-side, each player using two Stones, and playing each Stone alternately with his opponent. No player shall wear boots, tramps or sandals with spikes or other contrivance which may break or damage the surface of the ice. The rotation of play observed during the first Head of a Game shall not be changed. Any Rink not having its full complement of four players shall be disqualified, except in the case of illness or accident during the Game, in which case the Lead shall play four Stones.

55. The Skips opposing each other shall settle by lot, or in any other way they may agree upon, which side shall lead at the first Head, after which the winners of the preceding Head shall lead, and shall continue to do so if any extra Heads be played.

56. The Skip shall have the exclusive regulation and direction of the game for his Rink, and may play last Stone, or any position in the game he pleases. When his turn to play comes, he shall select one of his players to act as Skip in his place, and take the position of an ordinary player. He may, however, return to the tee for brief consultation with the acting Skip.

57. Players, during the course of each Head, shall be arranged along the sides, but well off the centre of the rink, and no player, except when sweeping according to rule, shall go upon the centre of the rink, or cross it when a player is about to play or when a Stone is in motion. Skips only shall be entitled to stand within the Circle. The Skip of the playing side shall have the choice of place, and shall not be obstructed by the other Skip in front of the Tee, while behind it the privileges of both, in regard to sweeping, shall be equal. No player other than the Skips acting for the time being may stand behind the Circle while play is proceeding.

58. Each player must play from the hack or crampit and, in the delivery of the stone, no part of the player's body or equip-

ment shall go beyond the nearest hog score during the uninter-
rupted motion in the delivery of the stone, *i.e.*, a player in the
act of delivering a stone must come to a complete stop before
any part of the body reaches the nearest hog score. Nor shall
the player be permitted to leap over, slide over on the other foot,
or even put his hand over to check his slide.

Left-handed players shall play from the hack or crampit
placed on the right-hand side of the centre line and right-
handed players shall play from the hack or crampit placed on
the left-hand side of the centre line. Stones delivered from the
wrong hack or crampit or by a player not complying with Rule
58 shall be removed from play by the playing side immediately
after the player has delivered his stone. Should the playing side
not remove the offending stone then the umpire shall have the
power to order the removal of said stone. However, if the stone
so played has come to rest or struck another stone, the played
stone shall be removed and the displaced stone or stones be placed
as nearly as possible where they originally were to the satisfaction of the opposing skip. Both skips should agree upon the position, but, failing agreement, the umpire shall decide. No player
may hold his stone and return to the hack or crampit for
another delivery once the stone has crossed the nearest sweeping
score : in the event of an infraction, the stone shall be removed
from the ice by the playing side.

59. Each player must be ready to play immediately when his
turn comes, and must not take more than a reasonable time to
play. Should a player play a wrong Stone, the Stone which
ought to have been played shall be put in its place.

60. If a player should play out of his turn the Stone so played
may be stopped in its progress and returned to the player.
Should the mistake not be discovered until after the Stone has
come to rest or has struck another Stone, the Head shall be continued as if it had been played properly from the beginning, but
the missed Stone shall be played by the player missing his turn
as the last Stone for his side for that Head. In the event of two
Stones being played in succession by one side in error, the Head
shall be declared null and void.

61. The sweeping shall be under the direction and control of the Skips. The player's side may sweep the ice from the Hog Score next the player to the Sweeping Score, and any Stone set in motion by a played Stone may be swept by the side to which it belongs. Skips only shall be allowed to sweep behind the Tee. When snow is falling or drifting, the player's side may sweep the ice from Sweeping Score to Sweeping Score. The sweeping shall always be to a side, and no sweepings shall be left in front of a running Stone. Both Skips have equal right to clean and sweep the ice behind the Sweeping Score, except while a player is being directed by his Skip. Skips shall not sweep behind the Sweeping Score until an opposing Stone reaches this Score. At the end of any Head, either of the Skips may call upon all the players to clean and sweep the entire rink. If objected to, this shall be subject to the approval of the Umpire.

62. (*a*) If, in sweeping or otherwise, a running Stone be touched by any of the side to which it belongs it shall be removed from the ice, but if by any of the opposing side it shall be placed where the Skip of the side to which it belongs shall direct. Should the position of any Stones be altered by such affected Stone, the Skip opposed to the side at fault shall have the sole right to re-place them.

(*b*) Should any played Stone be displaced before the Head is decided, it shall be placed as nearly as possible where it lay, to the satisfaction of the Skip opposed to the side displacing. If displaced by any other side both Skips should agree upon the position to which it is to be returned, but if they do not agree the Umpire shall decide.

63. All games shall be decided by a majority of Shots. A Rink shall score one Shot for every Stone which is nearer the Tee than any Stone of the opposing Rink. Every Stone which is not clearly outside the outer Circle shall be eligible to count. All measurements shall be taken from the Tee to the nearest part of the Stone. Disputed Shots shall be determined by the acting Skips; if they disagree, by the Umpire, or where there is no Umpire, by a neutral curler chosen by the Skips. No measuring of Shots shall be allowed previous to the termination of the Head.

64. If from any change of weather after a Match has been begun, or from any other reasonable cause, one side should desire to shorten the rink, or to change to another, and if the two Skips cannot agree, the Umpire shall, after seeing one Head played, determine whether and how much the rink shall be shortened, or whether it shall be changed, and his decision shall be final. In no case, however, shall the rink be shortened to less than 32 yards from the Foot Score to the Tee. Should there be no Umpire, or should he be otherwise engaged, the two Skips may call in any neutral curler to decide, and his powers shall be equal with those of an Umpire. The Umpire shall, in the event of the ice appearing to him to be dangerous, stop the Match. He shall postpone it, even if begun, when the state of the ice is in his opinion not fitted for testing the curling skill of the players. Except in very special circumstances, of which the Umpire shall be judge, a Match shall not proceed, or be continued, when a thaw has fairly set in, or when snow is falling and likely to continue during the Match, nor shall it be continued if darkness comes on to prevent the played Stones being well seen by players at the other end of the rink. In every case of such postponement to another day the Match, when renewed, must be begun *de novo*.

ROYAL CLUB COMPETITIONS

The following definitions shall apply to Royal Club Competitions:

Game: Play between two rinks by time or a given number of ends to determine a winner, or result.

Match: A contest of two or more rinks playing against an equal number to determine a winning side by total number of points or games.

Competition: A playdown by any number of rinks playing 'games' to determine a final winner. If there is more than one contest within a competition, as for first event, second event or more, each 'event' shall be considered a separate 'competition' under this paragraph.

The Competitions shall be played under the Rules of the game as approved by the RCCC except that the substitution of players shall be covered by the following :

Every Rink shall consist of four players, each player using two stones, and playing each stone alternately with his opponent. No player shall wear boots, tramps or sandals with spikes or other contrivance which may break or damage the surface of the ice. The rotation of play observed during the first Head of a GAME shall not be changed. In any game, match or competition, a Rink not having its full complement of four players shall be disqualified. When, owing to illness, accident or any valid reason, a player is unable to play in any round, he may be replaced by another player as substitute, provided this substitute has not already taken part in the competition in any other Rink. A substitute may play in any position in any round but not higher than the position of the curler he is replacing. The Skip shall declare any substitute in the first round of a competition or the Rink in the first round will be understood to be the entered Rink. No Rink shall take into play more than two substitutes in any game, match or competition. In the case of illness or accident to a player during a game, the lead shall play four stones, always provided that, if a substitute is available, he shall be played. All substitutes must be eligible in terms of the Rules of the Competition.

Grateful acknowledgement is made to the Royal Caledonian Curling Club for permission to reprint the Rules of Curling.

As previously stated, it is implicit in these Rules that they are interpreted in a sporting manner by curlers. Sportsmanship is the beginning and the end. Without it, curling is merely a technical exercise, a grouping of stones. With it, curling becomes a game with attributes of conduct and character which have earned for it the title, the greatest ambassador in sport.

The Rules most commonly broken, through ignorance, are :

57. 'Skips only shall be entitled to stand within the Circle' and 'No player other than the Skips acting for the time being

may stand behind the Circle while play is proceeding'. Keep your place on the ice!

58. (The 'Slide'): A number of curlers stand up after delivery but do not come to a complete stop and continue to move forward over the hog. Also 'Stones delivered from the wrong hack or crampit shall be removed from play by the playing side'. Too often, a curler plays from the hack in the wrong position; he should make certain that the hack is properly positioned before he plays, especially if members of the opposing rink are left-handed.*

59. 'Each player must be ready to play immediately when his turn to play comes.' Be prepared and don't waste time!

61. 'Skips only shall be allowed to sweep behind the Tee.' In modern curling, particularly in the take-out game, a skip often directs a player to strike a stone at the back of the house; when the shot is narrow, his sweepers frequently sweep past the Tee up to the back stone. This is wrong. The sweepers should stop at the Tee Score, when the skip may take over. Also 'Skips shall not sweep behind the Sweeping Score until an opposing Stone reaches this Score'. (This Rule was passed at the 1968 Annual Meeting of the Royal Club; prior to this, a skip could polish the ice while waiting for an opposing stone to reach the Tee Score but this was seldom done.)

THE POINTS GAME

The Game of Points, the individual curling game at which the curler scores for himself alone, is viewed from different angles by curlers. Some say it is a poor game compared with the real thing and will have nothing to do with it. Further criticisms are that team spirit is lost, that it is wrong for curlers to play without a broom to aim at and that it can be a boring business to wait in a queue to play.

* 'In 1820, a left-handed player was admitted a Member of the Club, and although an excellent curler, a condition was made that he should forfeit one gill of the best whisky every time he forgot to shift the board'. From the Minutes of the Largs Curling Club. (Today, it is encumbent on the player about to play to shift the hack.)

But, viewed in its proper perspective as a form of practice, 'Points' can give valuable basic training to beginners. A well-known American Curler, J. Nelson Brown of Detroit, added another dimension to the game when he wrote: 'The Points Game is the best tonic for the curler who has gotten too big for his britches and has the ill-conceived notion that he is far and above his fellow curlers.'

The argument that first-class curlers are not good at Points does not bear scrutiny. James Sellar, thought by many to have been, at his best, the top curler in Scotland, was also a master at Points. He compiled many scores in the forties and held the Merchiston Club's Points title from 1927 to 1955, a phenomenal run of 28 years.

Now 50 is the target and James Scott (Falkirk), Jack Lamb (Lesmahagow), Tom McGregor (Lesmahagow), Willie McIntosh (Findo Gask) and Robin Welsh (Watsonian) have broken that barrier, James Scott's 53 being the top score we know of in Scotland.* (Some high scores quoted in record books are 'eclectic' scores, compiled by adding together the best scores at various points in more than one attempt in the Competition. These should be disregarded.)

The ladies, who have humbled their menfolk on many occasions in Scottish competitions, have also shown their prowess at Points. Betty Law, Abdie Ladies, probably the best lady curler in the country, has a 47 to her credit.

A normal procedure at presentation ceremonies in Scottish Ice Rinks is to ask the winning skip to tell the assembled company how he did it – and his normal reply is that he was clever enough to place three better players than himself in his rink! But it is every man for himself, and every woman for herself, at Points. We now give the Rules and diagrams for Points play

---

* James Sellar, the Manager, who was connected with Edinburgh Ice Rink for 47 years until 1966, recalls that from 1912 to 1936 no one scored 40 at Points. Then, as in the four-minute mile, the barrier was frequently broken, once the elusive figure had been achieved. As we go to press we learn that James Stewart, Colmonell, has created a new record with a 57 at Ayr Ice Rink and that Jimmy Law has scored a 50 at Hamilton.

and challenge young curlers to make a name for themselves by beating their elders.

RULES FOR THE POINTS GAME

Competitors shall draw lots for the rotation of play, and shall use two Stones.

The measurement of the rink for Points Play shall be in conformity with the provisions of rule 43.

Two circles, one having a radius of 4 feet and the other having a radius of 6 feet shall be drawn round each Tee, and a line through the centre of each circle from the Foot Score to the Hog Score.

Every Competitor shall play four Shots at each of the nine following Points of the game, *viz.*: (1) Striking, (2) Inwicking, (3) Drawing, (4) Guarding, (5) Chap and Lie, (6) Wick and Curl in, (7) Raising, (8) Chipping the Winner, and (9) Drawing through a Port according to the definitions and diagrams here given.

In Nos. (2), (6), (8) and (9), and at (10) Outwicking when played, the object Stones shall be placed so that two Shots shall be played on the right at one Head and two on the left at the other Head.

No Stone shall be considered outside a circle unless it be entirely clear of that circle.

In the event of two or more Competitors being equal, they shall play four Shots at (10) Outwicking. If the Competition be still undecided, the Umpire shall order that one or more of the preceding Points be played again by the Competitors who are equal.

Note : Much time will be saved if two rinks be prepared lying parallel to each other, the Tee of the one being at the reverse end of the other rink; every competitor plays both Stones up one rink and afterwards both down the other, thus finishing at each round all his chances at that point.

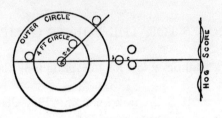

Placed Stones shown ●   Played Stones shown ⊙

1. Striking

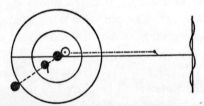

A Stone being placed on the Tee, if struck, shall count 1; if struck out of the outer circle, it shall count 2.

2. Inwicking

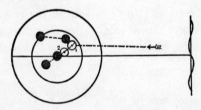

A Stone being placed on the Tee, and another with its inner edge 2 feet 6 inches from the Tee, and its fore edge on a line drawn from the Tee at an angle of 45 degrees with the central line, if the played Stone strike the latter on the inside, it shall count 1; if it perceptibly move both Stones, it shall count 2.

3. Drawing

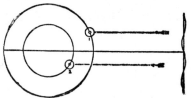

A Stone being played, if the same lie within or on the outer circle, it shall count 1; if within or on the 4-foot circle, it shall count 2.

4. Guarding

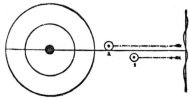

A Stone being placed on the Tee, if the Stone played rest within 6 inches of the central line, it shall count 1; if on the line, it shall count 2. It must be over the Hog, but must not touch the Stone to be guarded.

(For ease of measurement, score cards are six inches long.)

5. Chap and Lie

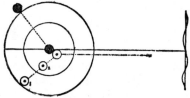

A Stone being placed on the Tee, if struck out of the outer circle, and the played Stone lie within or on the same circle, it shall count 1; if struck out of the outer circle, and the played Stone lie within or on the 4-foot circle, it shall count 2.

6. Wick and Curl in

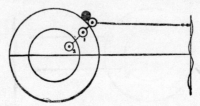

A Stone being placed with its inner edge touching the outer circle, and its fore edge on a line making an angle of 45 degrees with the central line, if the same be struck, and the played Stone curl on or within the outer circle, it shall count 1; if struck, and the played Stone curl on or within the 4-foot circle, it shall count 2.

7. Raising

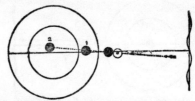

A Stone being placed with its centre on the central line and its inner edge 8 feet in front of the Tee, if it be struck into or on the outer circle, it shall count 1; if struck into or on the 4-foot circle, it shall count 2.

8. Chipping the Winner

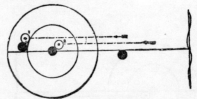

A Stone being placed on the Tee, and another with its inner edge 10 feet in front, just touching the central line, and half guarding the one on the Tee, and a third Stone being placed 4 feet behind the Tee, with its inner edge touching the central line, but on the opposite side from that on which the guard is placed, if the played Stone strike the Stone placed behind the Tee, it shall count 1; if it strike the Stone on the Tee it shall count 2. The maximum score for any one Shot shall be 2.

9. Drawing through a Port

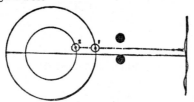

A Stone being placed with its inner edge on the central line 10 feet in front of the Tee, and another Stone on the opposite side and with its inner edge 2 feet from the central line, if the played Stone pass between these two Stones without touching either, and rest within or on the outer circle, it shall count 1; if within or on the 4-foot circle, it shall count 2.

10. Outwicking

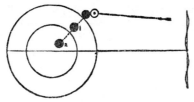

A Stone being placed with its inner edge touching the outer circle and its centre on a line making an angle of 45 degrees with the central line, if struck within or on the outer circle, it shall count 1; if struck within or on the 4-foot circle, it shall count 2.

CHAPTER SEVENTEEN

THE SKIP

THE SKIP, THE captain of the team, is the man all beginners must look to for guidance. This is a heavy responsibility for a skip and he should fulfil his obligations to his team members :

(*a*) By being decisive. Any uncertainty in giving directions is transmitted to his rink. He should not let the pace flag and become involved in 'committees'. Fast play, with brief consultations between skip and acting skip, is not only a Rule; it is also desirable for curlers and spectators.*

(*b*) By making each shot clear to his players. There should be no doubt what is required.

(*c*) By nominating simple shots. He should not complicate the issue with 'show' shots except in emergencies. To give a simple example, if there are three opposition stones in the house, a double take-out should be nominated (if all three stones go, so much the better).

(*d*) By giving his undivided attention to his players. We know of some skips who set the broom for a player and then turn their heads to light a cigarette or speak to other curlers.

---

* A touring Scottish skip reports that, on one occasion, he lit a cigarette and finished it while his opposition held a committee meeting to decide what shot to play. By no stretch of the imagination can many curling 'committees' be described as brief and the endless talk is so much hot air because a period measured in seconds not minutes is sufficient to sum up any situation in curling. Twelve ends of play should be easily attainable in a 2½ hour session. Some years ago, when consultations were not permitted, 16 to 18 ends were common, 21 ends possible, in a 3-hour game in Scotland.

(*e*) By giving credit to his players at all times for good shots *and* good attempts which fail, and by commiserating with players who are off form.

Most important of all, the skip should never lose his temper with his players (for their misses), with himself (for his misses) or with his opponents (for their successes with outrageous flukes). He must have fighting spirit and a keen determination to win but he must also be patient, calm and 'unflappable' or he will not be a good skip.

If he is a keen sportsman and has a sense of humour, all the other qualities should follow and he will also be a 'personality' who will keep team morale at a high level and earn the respect of his players. He will earn further respect if, after losing a game, he accepts responsibility and does not lay the blame at anyone else's door.

Encouragement of his team should be a skip's first aim. We have heard skips shouting, 'och, you're no' half-way,' and other terms of abuse to players after bad shots; have seen them throwing their arms to left or right to show how wide the shots were or throwing up both hands in despair; and have even seen them turning their backs on players.

Bad play is no excuse for a skip's bad manners which will also adversely affect his chances of victory. When trying hard to give of their best, players become anxious if they play badly and peevishness or ridicule will make them more anxious and less likely to recover their confidence.

In addition to encouraging his team members, a skip carries heavy responsibilities which weigh upon him from the very first stone. The first end is often vital. An opening offensive may take the opposing rink by surprise and a count of two or more shots can often dictate the whole course of the play. One way of stealing a march at the first end is to tell players before the game to be sure to be up on the new ice.

A skip must study the run of the ice at the early ends and quickly learn how stones run on either side of the rink and how the runs vary with different speeds of shot. Knowledge of the ice and strategy are the weapons used by the opposing skips in their personal war of nerves, and, given reasonable equality of play, games are won 'on the head' by skips who can 'read the ice' and apply their knowledge in strategic moves.

A ridge on the ice – once called a 'sow's back' – may force a skip to give minus-ice directions to his players. This means that a stone will fall back against the turn of the handle, and thus, in order to hit an opposing stone, the skip will place his broom in a position which appears to be on the wrong side of the stone. Such shots are normally played wide by beginners who find it difficult to believe that the fall-back, which seems un-natural to them, will be so considerable. Eventually, they will overcome this handicap and play the skip's broom with con-fidence. (On badly-prepared ice, fall-backs of up to six feet are occasionally experienced.)

The ability to read strange ice – away from their home Ice Rink, where they know every ridge and hollow – and knowing exactly when to sweep are other qualities of a good skip. One responsibility has been lifted from his shoulders. In the days before matched sets of stones, he had to learn the different properties of each pair of stones in his rink, one pair being duller than the others, one taking less turn and so on. But the skip must still learn the favourite shots, and the fads, of all his players and give instructions accordingly. Even top-class curlers, who, in theory, should be able to play all the shots with equal facility, prefer to strike, for example, on the in-turn, or have a predilection for a wick and roll rather than a draw.

The strategy of the skip is made up of a wide range of subjects, like switching from a striking to a drawing game and vice versa, cutting down on weight on swinging ice, keeping the front of the house clear when he has last stone, blanking ends to keep the last stone at the next end and the spreading of stones in the house when the opposing side is missing strikes. And we need not stress such elementary items as striking the front stone if two opposing stones are in the house and the truth of the old adage, 'the best guard is second shot'.

A skip has so much to think about that we hesitate to add

to his problems and will close this chapter on the duties of skips with one 'don't' and one 'do'.

Don't interfere with your third player or acting skip in any measurements or decisions needed at the conclusion of an end.

Do try to forget your previous misses during a game. Worrying about them is not worth a docken. Concentrate on the shot in hand and try your best; you can do no more.

CHAPTER EIGHTEEN

CONCENTRATION AND NERVES

... Low o'er the weighty stone
He bends incumbent, and with nicest eye
Surveys the further goal, and in his mind
Measures the distance, careful to bestow
Just force enough.
From Poems on Several Occasions *by*
James Graeme (Edinburgh 1773)

IN THE FINAL of the first Scottish National Schools Competition for the John Monteith Trophy, in 1967, Neil Turner, skip of the Glasgow High School rink, shouted at his players as they settled in the hack: 'Now, concentrate!'

Neil had the right idea, for concentration can be called the key-stone of curling. Many players are blessed with a natural ability, some have inherent 'touch', but a conscious effort is still required to play *every* shot.

It was said of Napoleon that he had many boxes in his mind and that he could close all but the one required to do the job in hand, eventually closing all to sleep. It was why his concentration was so intense, so remarkable even in the history of great men.

To apply such a mental approach is invaluable at all games, because each shot is then played as a separate entity unencumbered by thoughts of the bad shots which have gone before, the state of the game and what might follow. In the heat of a game, application of this kind is clearly difficult, but, with training, a curler can achieve a measure of detachment.

The first step towards this objective is to immerse yourself completely in your own game – not on the games on the adjoining rinks. Ken Watson, famous Canadian skip, reports

122

that one of the highest compliments ever paid his rink came from his opposite number in an important game: 'Gosh, Ken, I wish my men would quit watching the game on the next sheet. Your men are so busy watching every shot we make, I'll bet they don't know who is winning alongside us.' When asked, Ken's second player, Lyal Dyker, had to look at the scoreboard before answering.

Other aids-to-concentration are:

When you settle on the hack, clearly understand the shot required.

Keep your eyes fixed firmly on the skip's broom. (For 'keep your eye on the ball', the curler substitutes 'Look at the mark with all your een'.)

Swing the stone straight back, and, on the back-swing, sense the weight required for the shot.

Aim the throwing arm at the broom in a full and relaxed follow-through.

In other words, concentrate on the simple mechanics of delivering a curling stone.

Glenn Harris, former Editor of *The North American Curling News*, wrote on the subject: 'If a man will go through some sort of remindful ritual each time he prepares to deliver his stone, that will suggest concentration on the shot in hand, he'll improve his game at once.' *A remindful ritual*. The expression should become an essential curling term!

An apparently contradictory feature of concentration in any sport is that it must be allied to relaxation for tenseness cramps the style in every sense. But the anomaly is more apparent than real. To become immersed in a concentrated effort to produce your best is of itself a means of reducing tension.

All sportsmen worthy of the name have nerves. Without them, a champion could not lift his game to fit the occasion. Heroes are those with nervous temperaments who conquer or come to terms with their nerves.

Nervousness has little to do with lack of confidence. A good curler, for example, knows he can accomplish a given shot; he has done it dozens of times before. It is when the shot is called for in a crisis that nerves take over and panic ensues. The Canadians call shots of this nature pressure shots or 'the big ones' and we have heard many other names for them, some of them unprintable! Whatever name you use, they are the shots which win championships.

Conceit is a word we don't like in curling but the value of self-confidence cannot be stressed too strongly. If you look at a shot and feel you can do it, you very often will do it.

What can be done to help a curler when the crunch comes, when he faces the shot which matters more than any others in a game? The answer is nothing. He must help himself, by training and experience, so that, when the time comes to play the all-important shot, he is mentally equipped to meet the challenge.

Experience is the best-known cure for curling nerves but here are three hints which may prove helpful to beginners who feel nervous about a vital shot.

1. Be philosophical. After all, the worst that can happen is that the shot is missed.

2. Size up the situation calmly and resolve to make as good a shot as possible.

3. *Visualise* a successful shot.

CHAPTER NINETEEN

IT'S A SLIPPERY GAME

IN THE MODERN game, with its accent on high-powered play, the aim at the top level is to eliminate the element of chance. As few stones as possible are left in play – in case of a lucky rub or wick – unless a side is trailing, when, in need of shots, a skip must mix stones in the house in search of a big end.

But, at whatever level, curling retains the essential charm for which it is famous – the quick change of fortune which transforms a game and carries a team from the brink of defeat to dramatic victory.

The moral to be drawn, and it is one which curlers follow more and more as they gain in experience, is *never give up*. There are many aspects of a successful curler's make-up, but, if he is not imbued with an iron determination to fight on against the odds, he will never be a true champion.

Bob Dick, famous Glasgow curler whom we reckon to be the best player of his age anywhere – in his late 'eighties, he is still a redoubtable skip – follows a curling philosophy which should be adopted by all beginners : 'When you're up, don't smile too much; when you're down, keep smiling – you'll aye bob up again.'

When a very young curler, we played in a rink with three realists who gave us no chance in the final of a minor trophy against a crack rink. We quoted a line from one of John Masefield's poems : 'And the gold cup won by the worst horse at the races.' A poor line of poetry, it was a good line for the three realists. We won the cup.

The history of curling is punctuated by stirring stories of

victory against all the odds. When, more than 150 years ago, the Currie Club first drew up the system of play for the eight-points Points Competition, the Club President, the Rev. Dr Somerville, inventor of an improved form of crampit in 1833, said: 'we have now placed the Points Medal beyond the reach of duffers'. But, in the very first competition, the Medal was won by Willie Drum, whose distinction that day has been tarnished since as he appears in the record books as 'admittedly, the worst player in the Club'.

In our own day, there are memories which keep recurring, like the story told against himself by the well-known Scots curler, Horace Bell of the Panmure Club. 'I learnt a salutary lesson thirty-five years ago when we lay two comfortable(!) seconds before the opposing skip played his last stone. A cutting from the *Dundee Courier and Advertiser* reads: "A league game between Carnoustie Panmure and Dundee on the Dundee Ice Rink had an amazing finish. Panmure, skipped by Horace Bell, led 16.8 with one end to go. Dundee, skipped by P. T. Roberts, played a sensational last end, lying all eight shots to force a draw".' This may well be the only example of a last-end '8' to peel a game but it proves the truth of the old saying, 'you're never beaten until the last stone is played or you're nine down with an end to go'.

Bill Piper, three times a winning skip in the Scottish Championship at Perth, was involved in what is probably the most astonishing come-back of modern times. In a Perth *v.* Edinburgh inter-city match in Edinburgh Ice Rink in 1956, Bill lost a '6' at the first end and was 18.0 down after little more than an hour's play. Then the 'impossible' happened and, with a '6' at the last end, Bill won 21–19! The banter after that memorable game included this gem from the winning lead, Dr John MacDougall: 'we would have annihilated them if we had found the weight of the ice earlier!'

When down, even when well down, never give in. Often, late in the game, a chance comes for a big end, and, if you can take it, you will be back in the fight. Once there, it's the other side's turn to worry.

These examples of the two imposters, triumph and disaster – and every curler has his stock of miraculous escape-stories – make the the wise curler wary of an early lead, soon to be dissipated by the laissez-faire attitude of his own side or the inspired play of his opponents; and, once on the slide, how difficult it is to regain control!

The moral of this aspect of curling is *never let up*. When six shots up, try to become eight shots up. Don't relax. One careless stone can be the turning point in a game.

The ups and downs of curling build character. It was what the old curler meant when, admitting defeat at the hands of a much poorer rink, he said: 'Aye, it's a slippery game but it makes you stand on your own two feet!'

CHAPTER TWENTY

CURLING PRIZES

IN THE YEARS of competitive play in the indoor Ice Rinks in
Scotland until 1939, the greatest rink in the country was undoubtedly the famous Jackson rink from Symington, skipped
by W. K. Jackson and including his two sons, Laurence and
Elliot. Willie Jackson, who died in 1955, aged 84, was the best-
known Scottish curler of the inter-war period. He skipped his
all-conquering rink to success in no fewer than 59 competitions
in Edinburgh Ice Rink alone and scored many other triumphs,
including a runaway victory in the Winter Olympic Games at
Chamonix in 1924, the only time curling has been included as
a participation sport in the Games. Willie Jackson, skip, with
his son Laurence leading, and Robin Welsh and Tom Murray,
took the gold medals for Britain with easy wins over Sweden
and France.

The British curling deputation at the Games, led by Colonel
Robertson Aikman, President of the Royal Club, were as proud
of the medals and diplomas won as the four Scots who had won
them.

In the immediate post-war era, John Robertson and Bob
Dick of Glasgow, Laurence Jackson, James Sellar and Willie
Scobie of Edinburgh, Bill Piper and Tom Morris of Perth and
Willie Young and Alex Mayes of Falkirk were top skips in an
ever-widening competitive field. Willie Young and his rink –
John Pearson, James Scott and Bob Young – amassed a record
of wins in major competitions which elevated them to the peak
position held by the Jackson rink in the pre-war period.

During the transition from Willie Young's pre-eminence to
the modern scene, George Lindsay of Waterside was recognised

Above: A typical four-laned Ice Rink in the United States. Behind a glass partition the spectators or 'plate-glass skips', as they are called – comment on the play and never miss a shot! *Below:* Opened in Stockholm in 1967, this Ice Rink has a reinforced plastic covering, weighing three tons, which is kept in position by warm air fans. The construction costs are considerably less than for a conventional Ice Rink

Above: This picture of the 1964 World Championship for the Scotch Whisky Cup in Calgary illustrates the spectator support for the game in Canada. *Below:* Droukit! While playing on the Comrie pond at his estate in Perthshire, four years ago, Sir Robert Dundas, Bart., and his fellow curlers fell through the ice and were helped to the shore. The photographer, Mr. Cowper, also went through the ice while compiling a Television film, which ended dramatically with a sequence fading into the sky as the camera fell with the cameraman!

as one of the most dominant figures in the Scottish game, and, in recent years, the Perth rink skipped by Chuck Hay and Alex Torrance's Hamilton and Thornyhill Club rink, while being continually pressed by a growing group of top-class teams, have established themselves as the most successful rinks in Scotland. (The members of these two top teams are pictured in the photographic section.)

All these high-class sides, and others too numerous to mention, have left prize-giving ceremonies in Scottish Ice Rinks loaded down with cups and mementoes. It was once said of Willie Young at a closing function in Edinburgh : 'He'll need one of Jimmy Alexander's lorries to take his trophies home !'

But all Scottish trophies are returned for the competitions the following season and the winners are left with their individual prizes as memories of their victories. For this reason, we make a plea to all Ice Rink and Curling Club Committees to give prizes which, while not valuable items in themselves, will become valued mementoes to the winning players.

A replica of the trophy is excellent. So is a medal, suitably inscribed, containing the badge of the Ice Rink or Club. If glass or silver prizes are chosen, they assume curling significance if the name of the competition and the year is inscribed on them. Bear in mind that prizes will be placed in glass cabinets or trophy rooms in the winners' homes and that, in the years to come, old curlers will show their collection to friends, children and grand-children who will be much more impressed if the titles and years of competitions can be read. A number of jewellers display a wide range of attractive items with curling motifs and a gift of framed photographs of the winning team is another thought for committees who are preoccupied with problems of prizes.

There is a growing tendency to give bigger and 'better' prizes, often unconnected with the competition or the game of curling. The extreme cases are the Canadian car bonspiels which alter the whole aspect of the game. We Scots have been taught to shrug our shoulders at misfortune and to keep smiling in adversity. But playing for cars would tend to wipe the smiles

E

from our faces, for the shots that matter in a competition would matter much too much if there were limousines waiting beyond the tee.

The practice of giving expensive and exhibitionist prizes is out of keeping with the traditions of the game. Curlers have always taken the view that the honour of winning should be great, the prize small. They admire the cup but treasure the prize, which has little intrinsic value, but, later, much sentimental value.

The worst feature of the expensive prize is that, if one club offers it, the next club will feel that, to attract the best entry, it must follow suit and the insidious practice, once started, will spiral as clubs vie with each other in matters of finance and prestige, neither of which has anything to do with curling.

To the claim that bigger prizes make better curlers, we say that commercialisation may make the competition fiercer but there is bound to be a corresponding loss in the spirit of fun traditionally associated with curling events. To the question, 'but where do you draw the line?' we answer that those who cannot see the huge gulf between cars and cash on the one hand and Scottish prizes on the other must find it difficult to discern between the in-hand and the out-hand.

We are happy to think that the Jacksons, Youngs, Hays and Torrances of the curling world have sideboards groaning with miniature trophies, medals and mementoes – perennial reminders of their prowess on the ice and of last-end, last-gasp victories – and that their cars are their own. For the rest of us, with one or two medals, or none at all, it's still a great game!

CHAPTER TWENTY-ONE

OVERSEAS CURLING COUNTRIES

FAMOUS AS OVERSEAS settlers, Scotsmen have made 'their ain game' everybody's game. Their missionary activities in many lands have built curling into an international game and we devote a chapter to 'potted' histories of curling in fourteen countries, each one of which deserves a book to itself.

CANADA :

The game was introduced in Canada by early Scottish fur traders and by soldiers in Fraser's Highlanders after the Siege of Quebec in the latter part of the eighteenth century. Wearying for their national game, and finding ideal conditions in the hard Canadian winters, the soldiers melted down cannon balls and curled on the St Lawrence River. The curlers in Eastern Canada used 'irons' – cast-iron 'stones', with iron or brass handles, weighing around sixty pounds and these passed from the competitive scene only fifteen years ago.*

The Royal Montreal Curling Club, not only the first curling club in Canada but the first sporting club of any kind on the North American Continent, was founded in 1807 'by twenty natives of Scotland who wished to introduce their favourite game to the St Lawrence'.

In 1835, the first match between clubs in different parts of the country was played between Quebec and Montreal at Three Rivers. Quebec won 31.23 and the losers paid for the dinner,

---

* Irons were originally developed because of the difficulties and delays in procuring stones from Scotland in the days of sailing ships. Iron players concentrated on the Drawing Game.

after which the Montreal Secretary reported : 'As this is the first, so I hope it will be the last time that ever we shall hear of champagne being exhibited at a bonspiel dinner.' Colonel Dyde answered diplomatically that there was no good, not even tolerable, whisky to be had in Three Rivers !

The Canadian Branch of the Royal Caledonian Curling Club was founded in 1852 and a measure of its continued strength and authority can be gauged by the superb organisation at the World Championship for the Air Canada Silver Broom in Pointe Claire, Quebec, in 1968, when Bill Mackay, the Branch President, and his welcoming committee were congratulated by curlers and administrators from eight nations for a remarkable feat of organised planning at necessarily short notice.

But Western Canada, with its highly-competitive urge, has contributed most to the big Canadian curling boom in the last thirty-five years. The Canadian Championship for the Macdonald Brier Tankard, which was started in 1927, did not create large spectator interest until the mid 'thirties, but, since then, has become one of the wonders of the curling world.

The Canadian Curling Association, now the ruling body in Canada, estimates that 550,000 Canadians now curl, including schoolboys and casual curlers who play on a pay-as-you-play basis. The National Schoolboy event, started in 1950, was followed by the 'National Mixed' in 1964 and the 'National Seniors' in 1965. In November 1968, Canada's *Financial Post* reported that the sale of curling equipment, including stones, brooms, shoes, sweaters, trophies and even ice scrapers, brought in an annual total of 6,000,000 dollars. Canada, now easily the biggest curling nation, issued a curling postage stamp on 15th January, 1969.

No mention of Canadian curling by a Scot would be complete without reference to Brigadier Colin A. Campbell, Past-President of the Dominion Curling Association (the Association, formed in 1935, became the Canadian Curling Association in 1968), Chairman of the Canadian Committee in charge of overseas tours, Captain of the Canadian Team in Scotland in 1960, guide, counsellor and friend to Scottish touring teams in

Canada and a man famous, among many other things, for his 'morning and evening classes'* at gatherings of international curlers. Collie Campbell's immense service to curling was recognised by the Royal Club when, at the Annual Meeting in 1965, he was elected an Honorary Member, a position he holds with The Duke of Edinburgh. In March, 1969, he was further honoured when elected President of the International Curling Federation.

C. H. Scrymgeour is the hard-working and greatly-respected Secretary of the Canadian Curling Association.

UNITED STATES OF AMERICA :

In the wilds of Michigan in 1832, eight hardy Scots formed Orchard Lake Club, the first curling club in the United States. As they had no curling stones, they started with hickory blocks. The New England Club of Boston began before 1839 and other pioneering clubs were Milwaukee (1845) and Portage (1850); all three of them are still thriving. The Boston Club made arrangements with the Boston Arena around 1910 for three sheets of ice for curling and this is thought to have been the first indoor curling in America, although exhibition games were played in covered rinks in Brooklyn, New York, before the turn of the century. The Country Club, Brookline, built a four-sheet indoor Rink, opened in December, 1920, and this was the first American Ice Rink solely used for curling.

The Grand National Curling Club of America was established in 1867, David Bell, who hailed from Dumfries, being the first President. The Club celebrated its centenary two years ago, under the Presidency of Edward Childs, a much-travelled, highly-popular figure, and published a commemorative booklet containing a fascinating account of the history of American curling.

In 1957, the first United States National Curling Championships were held in the Chicago Stadium. The event was

---

* At these 'classes', Collie Campbell, resplendent in special curling aprons, dispenses his particular brand of refreshments, which require sacks of lemons, bags of sugar and considerable expertise. Curlers from many parts of the world will testify that Collie is the perfect barman.

sponsored by Hughston McBain of McBain, Walter Rhodes being the Promotion Chairman. The Hibbing rink from Minnesota, skipped by Harold Lauber, were the first national champions. Thousands of Americans saw the game for the first time.

Glenn Harris, who, as Editor of *The North American Curling News,* was an important contributor to the growth of the game in the United States, wrote in 1960 : 'Vast changes have come. Prior to the birth of the *News* in 1944–45, refrigeration for curling ice was practically unknown. Matched stones had hardly been thought of. In a great section of the country, curling clubs but a short distance apart were not aware that others existed.' Glenn Harris retired in 1960 and another active and articulate curler, L. T. 'Tink' Kreutzig, moved into the editorial chair.

In 1958, the United States Men's Curling Association was founded, with Walter Selck as President, and Walter Rhodes became President the following year. In the 1962–63 season, the Convener of the *Annual* Committee, Ray Meddaugh, prepared the first Association *Annual,* in which the President, Ralph Trieschmann, stated that the membership had grown to over 100 clubs.

The 1967–68 President, Joseph LeVine, reported : 'The steady growth of curling in the United States continues. Every State on the northern border of our country now has curling, from Maine to Washington (3987 miles). Add 500 miles to Alaska – we're really spread out! Of course, we have curling in the Central States too, Nebraska, Colorado, California, Illinois, for instance. With our National Championship Playdown limited to twelve rinks, it is obvious that we must have area playdowns among our twenty-three curling States. Bonspiel activity is tremendous. If you are an ardent Spieler, you can compete in a different one every week-end, and mixed bonspiels are increasing fast.'

In 1968, the United States Women's Curling Association, under their President, Mrs William C. Elwell, became members of the Royal Caledonian Curling Club.

SWITZERLAND :

Scots started the game in St Moritz almost ninety years ago and other early clubs were formed at Grindelwald (1899), Arosa (1900), Celerina and Murren (1909), Villars (1910) and Wengen (1911). The Swiss Curling Association was founded in 1942.

In 1914, there were twenty-four curling centres; now, over eighty offer an embarrassment of riches and curlers from many nations flock to Swiss resorts each winter. Less than twenty years ago, there were only six artificial Ice Rinks in Switzerland – in Zurich, Berne, Basle, Neuchatel and Lausanne; in 1960, there were thirty-seven and now there are well over 100. The growth of artificial ice in the mountain resorts began ten years ago.

About the time the late Dr Alex Dimtza – famous surgeon, curler and personality – was President of the Swiss Curling Association (1957–59), the game in Switzerland suddenly leapt in popularity. New clubs, given impetus by the spread of artificial rinks, increased the population of Swiss curlers to around 3,500 in the early 'sixties.

Swiss lady curlers are also a force in the land. The Grindelwald Ladies Club – of which Alex Dimtza's wife, Heidi, a leading lady player in Switzerland, is a member – was formed in 1952 with thirty members. Zurich (1954), Berne (1955) and Basle (1959) followed this lead and the Swiss Ladies Championship, started in 1964, attracts a representative entry. The Swiss now aim to encourage the younger generation.

A Swiss Team of 16 curlers made the first official tour to Scotland in 1963 and a Scots Team toured Switzerland in 1967. The Swiss magazine of the game, *Curling,* edited for many years by Erwin Sautter, a keen curler and tireless curling writer and photographer, also gave drive and direction to the Swiss game. In 1967, the national Association celebrated its twenty-fifth Anniversary in delightful fashion in Zurich, and, immediately thereafter, the Dietikon, Zurich, Zurich Crystal and Wallisellen Clubs in Zurich combined to make history by building the first air-conditioned curling stadium with four sheets of ice.

Switzerland has been called the curler's paradise because the sun so often shines from a blue sky. Last season, with the curling population rising to well over 5,000, Bernhard Truninger (President) and Johnnie Tschappeler (Vice-President), the ever-active figures at the head of the Swiss Curling Association, must have felt that the sun was shining brightly over the Swiss curling scene.

SWEDEN:

William Andrew Macfie, of the Macfie Sugar Refining Company of Greenock, who was born in Scotland in 1807, introduced curling to Sweden in 1846 at Uddevalla on the west coast. He formed the first curling club, the Bohuslanska Curling Klubben, on 5th March, 1852, and, in the 1860's, Oscar, the Crown Prince of Sweden, who was a curler, became Patron of the Club.

Only the nobility curled in Sweden in those early days but the game became more widespread when the first club in Stockholm, the Amatorerna Club, was instituted in 1901. A Scottish group visited Stockholm in 1913 and a new club was instituted under the patronage of the Crown Prince. A year later, curling started at Are, a sports resort which now holds the famous annual Are Week of curling.

The Swedish Curling Association was instituted in 1916, and, in 1923, a Swedish team made the first official tour to Scotland. In this team was Erik Akerlund – father of 'Totte' Akerlund, one of the best-known and most successful curlers in Sweden today – and, in the same year, he presented the Swedish Cup. Competition for this cup lapsed between 1936 and 1961 but the event, re-started in the 1962–63 season, then became the premier international competition in Sweden. Staged every second year, it is a large-scale event with many nations competing. When President of the Royal Club in 1965, Major Allan Cameron won the Swedish Cup with a Scots rink – Willie McIntosh, Tom Pendreigh and Ken Maclennan. Totte Akerlund won the 1967 competition and carried off the Cup presented by his father.

Swedish curlers made their second Tour to Scotland in 1963 and the Swedish ladies made their first tour here in November, 1968, proving themselves to be skilful and attractive players and scoring a narrow win – by 744 shots to 740 – over the Scots in a fourteen-day tour.

Competition is fierce in the Swedish Championship because the Swedes are competitive curlers. Proof of this is their record in the World Championship. Entering the competition in 1962, they learned fast, adopted the sliding, take-out game, and, in 1967, the Swedish rink, skipped by Bob Woods, reached the final at Perth. The big new Ice Rink in Stockholm will improve their play still further. There are about 5,000 curlers in Sweden today, yet, until recently in Stockholm and the south, ice rarely appeared before the New Year and the season closed in the middle of March, and, only fifteen years ago, there were less than 1,000 curlers in Sweden.

Per Odlund, President of the Swedish Curling Association in the years of transition, must take a great deal of credit for the recent surge of curling popularity. A first-class curler and administrator, he captained the touring Team in Scotland in 1963 and travelled widely on behalf of Swedish curling. It was fitting that his last act after many years of devoted service as the national President was to preside over an international gathering of 600 curlers at the Jubilee Dinner of the Association in the impressive Stockholm Town Hall in 1966.

Rolf Arfwidsson is now President and the Secretary is Sven Eklund. Both are tall, athletic men, both top-class curlers. An attractively produced instructional booklet by Sven was recently published; it will give added impetus to the game in Sweden.

NORWAY :

The Elverhae Club, which was admitted to membership of the Royal Club in 1880, had strong connections with the Scottish Club, Evenie Water, members of each club being honorary members of the other. The Hon. Mrs Arbuthnott was Patroness of the Elverhae Club. This is the first record of curling in Norway.

Norwegian curling began in earnest in 1954, when, accepting an invitation from the Norwegian Travel Association, four Scots curlers visited Oppdal. The Scots – Bill Piper, Gilbert McClung, Balfour Kerr and 'Bunty' McWhirter – were welcomed by Erik Schonheyder, who formed the Oppdal Curling Club. The visit also inspired the formation of a new club in Oslo, Rolf Christensen, the first President of the Norwegian Curling Association, being elected Chairman. In 1955, another Scottish visit was made by John Monteith, 'Bunty' McWhirter, Rab Mitchell and Courtenay Morrison to Geilo and the Geilo Club was founded. Rolf Christensen, who was educated at Glasgow High School, returned the compliment with a short tour in Scotland in 1958. In his rink were Chris Walter, Fefor, later to be Vice-Captain of the 1965 Norwegian Team in Scotland, and Erik Schonheyder, Oppdal.

John Monteith, who presented curling stones to Norway, returned to Geilo in 1958 and played a match against and made a broadcast with Rolf Christensen. Later that year, John Solheim, the conscientious Secretary of the Norwegian Association for ten formative years, reported increasing activity and the launching of the Nordic Bonspiel, which is now played in Norway one year and Sweden the next.

Responding to a Norwegian invitation, Major Allan Cameron led two Scots rinks on a short tour to Oslo, Lillehammer and Trondheim in 1964. The visit coincided with the tenth anniversary of the Oslo Club, founded after the Oppdal games in 1954. Enjoyable matches were played at Bygdoy Ice Rink against rinks from Oslo, Frogner, Bygdoy and Stabekk Clubs. The tour ended with warm hospitality at Trondheim. One of the main events of the 1967–68 season was the tenth anniversary bonspiel of the Frogner Club.

Rolf Christensen retired from the Presidency of the Norwegian Curling Association after almost ten years' service and was succeeded by Birger Mortensen, who captained the team which made the first large-scale tour in Scotland in 1965. At that time, there were only 500 curlers in Norway; the figure was doubled three years later.

Extensive travellers, Birger Mortensen and his wife, Gerd, who both work hard for Norwegian curling, are internationally known and admired by curlers. Presiding over a growing number of clubs and curlers, Birger was delighted to announce in 1968 that the first indoor Ice Rink in Norway would be opened at Asker, near Oslo. Gerd tried the game, immediately liked it, and, as the first lady curler in Norway, quickly spread the good news and the Oslo Ladies Curling Club was formed.

NEW ZEALAND :

The New Zealand Province of the Royal Club was formed in 1886 and Thomas Callander, a curler from the West of Scotland, was elected the first President. He was the driving force behind the early spread of curling in New Zealand and his efforts led to the founding of a club at Dunedin in 1873. A club was formed the same year at Mount Ida, where the prospects for curling were better at 2,000 feet. Palmerston curlers travelled fifty miles to play the first bonspiel in New Zealand against Naseby in 1879.

Gerald Dowling, Ranfurly, keen curler and faithful correspondent, gives this picture of curling at the other side of the world :

'Most of the clubs are bounded by the mountainous country of Central Otago, from Ranfurly west to Alexandra, and including our two main curling centres, Naseby and Oturehua. The Clubs include only men as we have not the facilities for taking in and training school boys, nor have we the keen indoor ice to make it easier for our fairer sex. As you can imagine, playing outdoors, the ice does deteriorate about mid-day on the warmer days and requires a good swing on the keen side. Later in the day, you will be taking the weight off on the drug side as the ice tightens. Of course, we always use a crampit, and are not able to add the finesse to our shots possible on indoor ice of consistent quality. Being outdoors in the colder atmosphere, we always shout our orders to team members. We also include the bottle of Scotch among our ice necessities.'

As long ago as 1896, New Zealanders bemoaned the brevity of the curling season and considered the need for 'a Glaciarium'. But there is no indoor curling ice and the game is played in rugged conditions on frozen dams. Gerald Dowling reports that, in the eighty years of the Province, bonspiels have been held in fifty-one years, forty of which have been in July and August.

When ice conditions are right, excitement rises as curlers from far-flung areas foregather on the ice. New Zealand curlers are strong traditionalists. After bonspiels, they enjoy 'Beef and Greens' and initiate their young curlers at well-organised Curlers' Courts. The winter of 1968 was one of the best in recent years, ice on the larger dams lasting for a month. The twenty-six New Zealand clubs are in good heart. The Province President in 1968 was James Becker. The enthusiastic Secretary is Terry McKnight, Oturehua.

FRANCE :

French curling began in isolated groups early this century. But the French influence on Scottish curling was strong 150 years ago for we read, in John Cairnie's *Essay* (1833) that, among his favourite stones were Napoleon, Belle Poulle, Ca ira, La Liberté, La Forte and La Fidelle !

The Winter Olympic Games at Chamonix in 1924 led the tributaries of curling in the Haute Savoie area into one river and the 'channel' of this river was the French Championships which began at this time and have been held ever since.

There are now fifty clubs in the mountains of Haute Savoie and this is the stronghold of French curling. But the French game is moving purposely forward and we hear of curling at Lyons and in Paris itself. In 1968, the 'Challenge de l'Amitié' Competition was held by the Curling Club de Paris at the Charenton-le-pont Ice Rink in Paris, between rinks from Megeve, Chamonix, Mont d'Arbois, Saint-Gervais (Haute Savoie), and Swiss rinks from Crans-sur-Sierre, Lausanne and Montana; and Saint-Gervais staged the first Summer Tournament in 1968, pebbled ice being used for the first time in France.

The Auld Alliance between Scotland and France was further strengthened when a French team made a whirlwind tour of Scotland in November, 1968, the two French rinks playing in thirteen Scottish Ice Rinks in fourteen days. During the arduous tour, the French captain, Dr Albert Mure, and his team kept smiling and won a host of friends. A Curlers' Court was held at the Closing Dinner of the Tour, with Tom Stewart, Royal Club President-Elect, as 'My Lord', and the eight Frenchmen are now the only 'made' curlers in France.

Albert Mure, President of the Curling Committee of the French Federation of Ice Sports, a keen curler with a keen sense of humour, is at the head of French curling. His Secretary is Pierre Catella. Both men attended the first Air Canada Silver Broom Competition in Pointe Claire, Quebec, in 1968, and met curlers from eight nations.

ITALY :

An advertisement at the back of Bertram Smith's *The Shilling Curler* (1912) proclaimed Cortina d'Ampezzo as 'the Garden of the Gods' and offered curling in a skating rink of 25,000 square feet with excellent Scottish curling stones.

In his book, *The Complete Curler* (1914), J. Gordon Grant wrote of Cortina : 'The village with the surrounding cottages contains 3,000 inhabitants of a hard-working, simple-hearted, honest race. It has a post and telegraph office, library, doctor, chemist, excellent guides and English Divine Service during the season. Special attention is drawn to a Vienna Café where drinks, harmless or inebriating, are served at all hours of the day and night. About the prices, travellers can come to an understanding with the hotel proprietor ! The management and service are first-rate and entirely done by nice bright girls in Tyrolese costumes.'

Curling was revived in the wonderful setting 5,000 feet up in the Dolomites by the late Leo Menardi, a vibrant sporting personality who was the first President of the Cristallo Club and whose wife now carries on the curling tradition created by him. The Miramonti Club followed in 1955 with Federico Manaigo as President.

As in France, the holding of the Winter Olympic Games – in Cortina in 1956 – provided a springboard for development. Cortina was placed boldly on the curling map with the imaginative idea of holding a Summer Bonspiel on the Olympic ice. The first Bonspiel was held in June, 1958, and James M. Fleming, a keen Edinburgh curler and outstanding organiser, was invited to act as Umpire and assist on the planning committee. James Fleming described the event, which included five major competitions in a week, as 'a curler's dream come true'. Curling under a June sun continues to be one of the principal attractions at Cortina.

AUSTRIA :

James Fleming was also a tower of strength at Kitzbuhel, in the Austrian Tyrol, where, as in Cortina, curling had been played to some extent before the First World War. When the Kitzbuhel Curling Club was founded in 1955, James Fleming was the Club's representative member, and, for a number of years before his death in 1962, he stayed in Kitzbuhel to organise the curling at the height of the winter season. Baron Carl Menshengen provided three curling rinks alongside the skating rink, and in 1967 the Tourist Office built an artificial Ice Rink.

A famous ski-ing resort, Kitzbuhel soon became a noted curling centre, attracting an international gathering of curlers for a full programme of competitions from mid-December to early March; and, when the weather was bad for ski-ing, curling gained many 'converts'. Curlers from the Royal Canadian Air Force bases in Europe, many of them first-class players, frequented Kitzbuhel and mingled with winter sportsmen from many nations in a valley renowned for its mountain scenery.

Other resorts in the Tyrol started small curling clubs but Kitzbuhel, described in the travel brochures as 'The Ace of the Alps', is the capital of curling in Austria.

GERMANY :

David Lampl, who skipped the German rink when Germany first played in the World Championship at Perth in 1967, reports that curling was first introduced to his country in 1931. The occasion was the World Championships for a number of winter sports at Oberhof, Thuringia. In order to enlarge the winter sports atmosphere, the Archduke of Coburg-Gotha invited Scots curlers to play a game on natural ice and brought an ice-master from Grindelwald in Switzerland to prepare the ice. David Lampl began his curling career on this ice at Oberhof. Three rinks were laid but the ice lasted for only fourteen days and the Archduke concluded that the climate at Oberhof was not cold enough for curling.

Rolf Klug, second player in David Lampl's rink at Perth in 1967, advises us that Roman Roussell, a keen German curler who had learned to curl in Switzerland, met James Fleming at Kitzbuhel and persuaded him to help with the organisation of the first curling tournament at Garmisch-Partenkirchen in 1961. This was the beginning of modern curling in Germany.

Carry Gross, later President of the German Curling Association (instituted in March, 1966), and Mr Bruggemann launched a curling competition at Oberstdorf in 1962, and Adolf Hebeisen, a well-known Swiss curler from Thun, organised the event. Thereafter, a chain of competitions was created – at Garmisch-Partenkirchen, Bad-Tolz, Oberstdorf and Dusseldorf.

The Chairman of the German Association, Werner Fischer-Weppler of Munich, reports a growing number of German clubs and competitions – the most important of which is the international championship at Garmisch with forty rinks from seven countries. In 1968, there were 250 curlers in Germany, fifteen per cent of which were ladies.

BELGIUM :

The foundation stone of curling in Belgium was laid by Madame Jenny Francis in 1964. Madame Francis started to curl in Switzerland, at Murren, and presented a trophy there. She returned to her native land, imbued with the spirit of the game, and, largely through her efforts, the Curling Club Liège was founded, ice being obtained on Friday nights in the local Ice Rink. The organising zeal, and charm, of Madame Francis also led to the first Curling Championship of Liège, which was established in 1964 as an annual event.

In 1961, a group of enthusiastic Dutch curlers founded the Amsterdam Curling Club, the first curling club in Holland. Games were played on a new outside artificial ice stadium, specially built for speed skating, one of the most popular winter sports in Holland. The cost for play in this rink was considerable and the humidity of winters in Amsterdam posed additional problems. But the hard core of enthusiasts persevered, meeting twice a week for play. Winter holidays in Swiss resorts and curling in Scotland, at Edinburgh and Dundee-Angus Ice Rinks, kept the interest of members at a high level.

In 1966, S. Waterman, Secretary of the Club, wrote that, to improve their play, members were examining ways and means of building an indoor Rink but the cost of such a venture was too much for the forty members to bear.

The position is the same today. The Dutch curlers form touring teams and enjoy bonspiels in other lands while hoping to improve their position at home.

DENMARK :

The good news from John Christiansen, Secretary, was that the first club in Denmark, the Copenhagen Curling Club, had been formed and that it had enjoyed 'a nice accession after a great deal of publicity in the Press and on Television'. The club hired a big Ice Rink with space for five sheets of curling ice.

John Christiansen appealed to the Royal Club for curling stones (after a visit to Copenhagen by Bill Robertson Aikman, Royal Club President, and the Royal Club Secretary, in 1966, a supply of stones, many gifted by John Monteith, was shipped to Denmark) and for general information on curling as, in

John's words: 'We have been plunged headlong into "battles" against neighbouring towns without knowing the most elementary rules.'

We are sure the Copenhagen curlers now have the rules at their finger tips. The important part of the Danish letter came in the last paragraph: 'As you can see, the material side of the matter does not promise well. However, the will and the spirits are 100 per cent in order!'

Early in 1968, the Copenhagen Club held its first international bonspiel, for the Mermaid Cup, the entry including Swedish, Norwegian, Swiss and Danish rinks, and one Scots rink – Alan Johnston, James Hamilton, Jim Morrison and Sandy Aitken. Erik Mangor, the Club Treasurer, reports that there are now forty-five members who tour extensively and play a number of major events in Copenhagen.

JAPAN:

The late Dar Curtis, who spent many years and made considerable contributions on behalf of curling – he donated the Ice Rink at Wilmette, Illinois, now a civic curling centre – went to Japan with his wife, Happy, in February, 1967. In Tokyo, they demonstrated the art of curling to large crowds of interested Japanese and Dar Curtis, America's curling ambassador, sent this report of a successful mission:

'We feel sure you will be interested to learn that soon the Japanese nation may qualify as a member of our great world-wide fraternity of curlers. The first demonstrations and lessons we have given to many of these sports-minded people have been received with great enthusiasm. Thousands have turned out to see the "strange" Scottish sport which we feel sure is getting 100 per cent acceptance and will become one of the great "family" games of the country.'

Bearing in mind to what an extent the sports-loving Japanese have adopted golf – Scotland's other sporting gift to the world – we can only surmise what will happen if they take to the curling ice.

Curling has also been played in *Ireland* – in 1839, the celebrated John Cairnie was instrumental in founding the Belfast Club (which had a close connection with the Ardrossan Club in Scotland) and later clubs were started, in 1879, at Clandeboye and Kiltonga, Newtonards, but nothing was heard from Irish curlers after 1900; in *Australia* – William G. Moffat-Pender, assisted by fellow-Scots Dr Cyril McGillicuddy and Robert Jackson, started curling in the old Glaciarium in Melbourne in 1936, but Moffat-Pender, who was also a champion Highland dancer, died in 1939 and his friends died during the war; in *Russia* – the Moscow Club was established by a Scot, William Hopper, in 1873 and he and Lord Dufferin, the British Ambassador at St Petersburg, tried to found a St Petersburg club with the prospect of a 'curling congress' on the Neva (the Moscow Club continued until the First World War); and *China* – in 1966, Ernst Debrunner, Treasurer of the Swiss Curling Association, scratched his head in astonishment when he discovered curling stones in Tientsin (they were used by members of the Tientsin Club, which, instituted in 1890, thrived until the Second World War.)

CHAPTER TWENTY-TWO

OVERSEAS TOURS

IN FORMER TIMES, Scottish curlers undertook the perilous journey on foot over the snow-capped hill to play a challenge bonspiel against the neighbouring parish. In 1847, Charles Cowan, a distinguished curling administrator, urged curlers to travel by train in an article, *Prospective Advantages of Railways for Curlers,* in which he advised that 'sheets of shallow water be procured in juxtaposition with leading lines of railway'.

Now we fly in comfort to all parts of the curling world and travel to Switzerland more quickly than many an old-time curler took to reach the bonspiel in the next valley. The growth of overseas curling tours constitutes a revolution in the history of the game, which ranks in importance with the rounding of the stone and the invention of artificial ice.

'The curlers of Canada would be glad to play a friendly game against players from Scotland, if such a match could be arranged for next winter, and to ascertain on what terms such a challenge would be accepted.'

This invitation, from the Canadian Branch of the Royal Club, was sent to Scotland as long ago as 1858. A Scottish committee was formed, and, the following year, one of its members wrote: 'Our brethren in Canada appear to be disappointed that we have not yet accepted their challenge, but they may rest assured that nothing could give us more pleasure than having a meeting with them, and we hope a good time is coming, either for us going *there,* or for them coming *here.*'

David Mair, Secretary of the Canadian Branch, sent another letter, couched in more challenging terms: 'It surely cannot be that the Scotchmen are afraid of us! I am confident we could

find two rinks in Canada who would be willing to cross and
try what they could do.'

There was talk but no action. The Canadians, joined by the
Americans, persisted, and, in 1878, the Secretary of the Ontario
Branch of the Royal Club and the President of the Grand
National Curling Club of America sent separate invitations for
Scots teams to tour Canada and the United States. Circulars
were sent to Scottish Clubs but, again, no tour materialised.

Correspondence continued in sporadic fashion for a further
twenty years until, in 1901, Dr Barclay came from Montreal
to make a personal plea at the Royal Club Annual Meeting.
This galvanised the curlers of Scotland into action and an
advertisement calling for volunteers was inserted in the Press.
Over 200 applicants embarrassed the selection committee who,
after much heart-searching, chose twenty-eight curlers and
appointed the Chaplain, the Rev. John Kerr, as captain of this
first-ever Scottish Team to tour overseas. The team sailed for
Canada in December, 1902.

After a three-months Tour, the captain reported on the over-
whelming hospitality received from Canadians at every stage of
the journey and added that, wherever the tired Scots went,
they found a fresh relay of Canadian curlers waiting to receive
them 'with their feet, as it were, upon their native heath'. It
has been the same ever since. It is why the curlers of the host
country will always start favourites.

The captain gave one interesting reason for this first Canadian
victory : 'Our curling stones, while being transferred from place
to place in the railway trains that were heated to such a high
temperature, became themselves over-heated and required a considerable time to cool down. On more than one occasion the
members of the team were surprised to find their curling stones
settling down half-way up the rink when they had given them
sufficient impetus to carry them into the "parish", and on going
up to find out the reason for such conduct, it was found that by
their extra warmth the stones had embedded themselves to a
considerable depth in the ice.'

The Canadians made their first Tour to Scotland in 1909

and veteran curlers still remember the excitement caused by the arrival of the 37 tourists in Edinburgh. The atmosphere of anticipation was heightened by Mr Maitland, the station master at Waverley Station, who placed fog signals on the rails leading to the main platform and loud reports heralded the approach of the visitors.

Amid scenes of wild enthusiasm, a pipe band led a long procession into Princes Street *en route* to the North British Hotel. The next day, a specially decorated train took the Canadians to Peebles, where they planted a maple tree in the public park. They marched in torchlight procession with members of the Upper Strathearn Province. Novel and elaborate plans were made at every stopping point on the tour to welcome the visiting team.

Over 500 curlers attended the Tour Banquet in the Music Hall, Edinbugh, under the chairmanship of Lord Strathcona and Mount Royal, President of the Royal Club, who presented the Strathcona Cup for competition between the two countries.*

There were two particular personalities in that first Canadian Team – the team captain, the Hon. Duncan Cameron Fraser, Lieutenant-Governor of Nova Scotia, 'an exceptionally tall figure with strong Celtic features, whose splendid oratory touched all hearts and set the whole gathering aglow with enthusiasm;' and C. W. Macpherson, 'possibly the cheeriest tourist,' who travelled 7,000 miles to reach Scotland from Dawson City in the Yukon, starting his journey on a dog sledge!

A Royal Club Team, captained by John Watson, President, went to the United States in 1955, following the first Tour by American curlers in Scotland in 1952. John Watson and the nineteen members of his team were, in John's words, 'photographed, televised, feted, bagpiped and generally overwhelmed with kindness'. Team members called the tour 'the experience of a lifetime'. The Scots won the Trophy, presented for com-

---

* The Cup has been won six times by Canada, five times by Scotland, in subsequent exchange tours. The countries now play every five years and the Canadians will tour Scotland again in January, 1970.

petition between the countries by Commander Herries Maxwell, Royal Club President in 1950–51, and gained countless admirers with the accuracy *and speed* of their play. Glenn Harris, Editor of *The North American Curling News*, reported: 'The Scots curl concisely, quickly – and no foolin'. No time-consuming decisions in the "head", no lengthy consultations on the shot to play.' Tours with the United States are now on the same basis as tours with Canada – a five-year home-and-away programme – and American curlers will visit Scotland again in 1972.*

The lady curlers of Scotland made history when they toured in Canada and the United States in 1958.† Captained by Jean Gow, wife of that year's President of the Royal Club, Brigadier Jack Gow, the sixteen Scots became front-page news. These newspaper 'quotes' give a hint of the atmosphere of that first ladies tour, in which the Scots beat Canada by 486 shots to 396 and U.S.A. by 403 shots to 264:

'Perhaps it was the bagpipes, perhaps the fine dinner and certainly the entertainment by Peterborough lady curlers which helped the Scots to relax and later show their natural vivacity as eight of them clicked heels and hooted in a Scottish reel. Mrs Nicol from Fife sang *Mary's Wedding,* with her country-women joining her in each chorus.'

'The Ottawa Curling Club became a wee bit of Scotland when the team of Scots was entertained to lunch. These ladies from the land where curling originated were colourfully arrayed in tartan skirts, heavy sweaters and tam o'shanters trimmed with pins. The ladies all wore their own tartans, which, unlike their names, do not change with marriage.'

Muriel McPherson, the Scottish Secretary, echoed the sentiments of Arthur Frame, Secretary of the 1957 Team in Canada,

* The Scots are unbeaten in the Herries Maxwell Trophy games, having been victorious in Scotland in 1952 and 1962, and in the United States in 1955 and 1967.

† Three years before, in 1955, eight Canadian and eight American ladies toured Scotland under the joint captaincy of Mrs H. L. Liffiton (Canada) and Mrs Horace Vaile (U.S.A.).

who remarked on his return : 'All tourists should pack a case of sleep !'

The first large-scale international match in history was played between Canada and the United States at Buffalo, Lake Erie, on 5th January, 1865, with over 200 curlers involved in a five-hour struggle. James S. Lyon, the chairman at the dinner after the memorable day said : 'Battle was fought on the dividing waters between the United States, during the Presidency of Abraham Lincoln, and Canada, in the twenty-ninth year of the reign of the glorious matron, Queen Victoria.'

The following day, the *Buffalo Express* reported : 'The watery line which separates us from our Canadian neighbours is bridged over by reciprocal friendship. We gracefully accept a handsome defeat. True, it may be that the superior practice of our Canadian friends resulted in our discomfiture, but what of that? The result has been a genial meeting, beneficial to both States, and pleasant to all curlers.'

Genial meetings, beneficial to both sides and pleasant to all curlers. The Buffalo newspaperman summed up not only the first tour but the succeeding tours by all curling nations. An overseas tour is, truly, 'the experience of a lifetime,' in which curlers feel the glow of fellowship, and enjoy the fun and rich humour which goes with it, including the inevitable *faux pas* which the perpetrator is never allowed to forget !

CHAPTER TWENTY-THREE

THE LADIES

ON HIS RETURN from the first Scots Tour to Canada in 1903, Major Scott Davidson of Cairnie, Fife, was given an enthusiastic welcome-home dinner in the Marine Hotel, Elie. Headed by a piper, a procession of fifty curlers, led by Sir Ralph Anstruther and Sir Archibald Campbell, marched into the dining-room to honour the returning hero in the name of the Hercules Club, in which he was a prominent skip.

In a survey of his tour, the gallant Major said: 'The ladies were particularly attentive. Indeed, I might have been married three or four times! He read out telegrams received *en route* through Canada, to prove the point:

'Absence makes the heart grow fonder' (from Maudie, Halifax); 'Will ye no' come back again? All hearts bowed down' (from lady curlers, Montreal); 'None but the brave deserve the fair' (from Ethel, Winnipeg); 'I am still trusting' (from Mary).

It was particularly apt that the members of the Hercules Club should hear of the activities of lady curling enthusiasts in Canada for the Hercules Ladies Club, the first all-ladies curling club in Scotland, was formed in 1895 with Major Scott Davidson's wife as Vice-President.*

Only five years before, the Rev. John Kerr stated: 'Ladies do not curl. The Rational Dress Association has not yet secured for women the freedom that is necessary to fling the channel-

* The Ontario Curling Association report that the first ladies curling club in Canada was formed in Montreal in 1900 with 80 members, 'who curled every morning except Sunday'.

stone ... and the majority find the stones too heavy for their delicate arms.'

The author himself pointed out that there were several exceptions. There was a ladies bonspiel on Loch Ged in the Parish of Keir in 1840, when two rinks of the maidens of Capenoch played two rinks of the maidens of Waterside, and an enormous concourse of spectators watched the maidens finish the match up to their pretty ankles in water. Club Minute Books contain records of matches last century between married and unmarried ladies and between the married ladies of neighbouring parishes.

In 1884, the Hon. Mrs Fergusson opened the Pitfour Curling Pond 'with a stone of 36 pounds weight and delivered the same in true curling style, sending it the full length of the rink with such unerring aim that it drove a stone on the tee to the bank and lay itself a perfect pat-lid'. Her Ladyship's chap-and-lie shot was greeted with a vociferous cheer – and rightly so, for, apart from the excellence of the shot, she must have been a good sport to 'have a go' at what was then almost exclusively a man's game.

As John Kerr inferred, the long dresses of the Victorian era must have been an encumbrance even for lady athletes, and, for many years of the present century, ladies were regarded as something of a novelty on the curling rink.

Bertram Smith, in *The Shilling Curler,* wrote : 'For ladies – I am told – a straight-cut, fairly tight skirt is almost a necessity, otherwise the swing will be impeded.' This casual approach, in 1912, indicates that little attention was paid to lady curlers before the First World War.

Now ladies are seen everywhere on the ice and are welcome everywhere. What were the reasons for the change? One was the building of indoor Ice Rinks. Mrs Ruth Menzies, Honorary President of the Ladies Branch of the Royal Club, provides a second, significant reason.

Mrs Menzies started curling in 1919. In 1922, she became Secretary of the Edinburgh Ladies Curling Club, a position she held with distinction until 1959. The Club is believed to have been founded in 1912 but the first records start in 1915, when

Lady Marjorie Mackenzie presided over forty-five members. Lady Marjorie, Mrs Alan Menzies, Mrs Sang and Mrs Archie Leslie formed the nucleus of the club in these first years, when the ladies played with small black Crawfordjohn stones, some of which weighed less than 30 pounds. Edinburgh and Glasgow started ladies inter-city matches in 1930 and Mrs Menzies gives Glasgow credit for the change from small stones to man-size stones, which, she believes, was the fundamental reason for the big expansion and improvement in ladies curling.

Scottish Ice Rink Managements love the ladies! The large and ever-growing number of ladies clubs fill the ice in the morning and early afternoon sessions and make a valuable contribution to healthy balance sheets.

The ladies now march shoulder to shoulder with the men. In 1961, the Ladies Branch of the Royal Club was formally established under the Presidency of Mrs Jean Gow, who was followed, in 1963, by Mrs Irene Cleland, and, in 1965 by Mrs Janie Love. Outstanding curlers, they also proved themselves to be persuasive and efficient administrators. The organisation continues to flourish and expand under conscientious office-bearers.

The ladies conduct all the business of the Branch, including the organisation and financing of overseas Tours, under the friendly banner of the Royal Club. Their 'delicate arms', if no less feminine than in 1890, have taken a firm grip of curling affairs.

CHAPTER TWENTY-FOUR

YOUTH AND AGE

ONCE CALLED, WRONGLY, an old man's game, curling is now, at the top level, essentially a young man's game. But the important thing is that, at many different levels, it is a game for all ages.

Old curlers continue to curl, sweeping less but using their heads more, until very late in life and there are many instances of curlers playing when over 90. 'In our club's history,' wrote Robert Goodwin of the Kirkintilloch Club in 1889, 'we have *conclusive evidence* that the game of curling tends to a life of good health and length of days.'

In Edinburgh in the 'thirties, there was an annual match – for walking sticks! – between the over-65's and over 70's, many of whom were over 80. A curling span of 50 or 60 years is common in Scottish curling. It is the same overseas; ten years ago, at a bonspiel in Milwaukee, a photograph was taken of five American curlers, all of whom had curled for more than 50 years – David Bogue, Portage (64), Stephen Dooley, Milwaukee (58), Louis Ehlert, Milwaukee (55), Ferge Ferguson, Milwaukee (54) and Robert Stevenson, Waltham (52).

At the other end of the scale, Scottish curling history contains a fair number of references to early attempts to encourage youth, the prime examples coming from the Sanquhar, Kilmarnock and Wanlockhead Clubs, all in the South-West of Scotland, for long a hot-bed of curlers. In his *History of the Sanquhar Curling Society* (1874), James Brown records that, in addition to the regular rinks in the early years of the Society (founded in 1774), there was a 'corps-de-reserve', composed of youngsters who were presided over by an experienced officer appointed at annual meetings.

A Kilmarnock curler wrote, in 1833, that his club had long been distinguished 'for the urbanity of its demeanour towards its juniors' and that the Junior Club had, from its formation, 'been remarkable for its indomitable perseverance and daring'. He added that the more recent Morning Star Club, an aptly named school 'for training the youth of our town at once to habits of early rising and the mysteries of the curling craft', met on the ice at 7 a.m., broke for coffee at 8 a.m. and curled until 10 a.m. when the members returned to business so that their elders could take over on the ice.

In 1912, at a dinner of the Wanlockhead Curling Society (founded in 1777), a speaker remarked that the Wanlock men were good curlers because they *learnt young*. Schoolboys had always been encouraged, he added, but the junior club, formed in 1883, had taught them to play regularly and properly and they now played like men and gentlemen.

The youthful urge in the country clubs faded with the advent of the big indoor Rinks, and, in 1961, we wrote: 'At the moment, our only answer to the immense reservoir of youthful talent in Canada is the T. B. Murray Trophy,* which, largely due to the efforts of Jock Waugh, well-known Scots curler and Director of the international Scotch Cup Competition, reverted two years ago to its original aim – to encourage competition between youngsters of 25 years and under. But this is almost the only bright spot in a black landscape. In recent years, Glasgow has introduced schoolboy curling, but, by and large, the junior position is little better than it was before the war.'

Schoolboy curling in Glasgow started in the early 1950's, when Arthur Frame, Secretary of the Glasgow Province, led boys from his old school, Hutcheson's Grammar School, on to the ice. Boys from Glasgow High School joined them and modern Scottish schoolboy curling was born.

Edinburgh followed this lead in September, 1961. A deputa-

* This Trophy was presented in 1929 by Tom Murray of Biggar, President of the Royal Club in 1936–37 and one of Scotland's best curlers. It was presented to the Royal Club by the Edinburgh Ice Rink Curling Club in 1959

tion of Watsonian Curling Club members met Mr Roger Young, Headmaster of George Watson's College, who readily agreed that a Watsonian curler should address the senior boys after Prayers on a Monday morning – an ordeal, the curler later confessed, far more nervewracking than throwing the last stone on which all depended. The response was at once a source of encouragement and embarrassment, 57 boys handing in their names for the school curling club. Watsonian curlers, given valuable assistance by Gilbert McClung, President of the Royal Club in 1962–63, Willie Scobie of the Corstorphine Club, and David Kennedy, Ice-Master at the Edinburgh Ice Rink, took eager groups of boys to the hacks. Gilbert McClung described the activity on the ice as 'the bravest sight in Edinburgh for many years'.

The first schoolboy inter-city match in Scotland was played between Glasgow and Edinburgh in December, 1961, Hutcheson's rinks beating Watson's in the Scottish Ice Rink, Glasgow, which provided what was described as 'a regal high tea' to round off a happy day.

Since that historic meeting, schoolboy curling has shot to the forefront in Scotland. Glasgow boys play in an inter-schools league on Saturday mornings. In Edinburgh Ice Rink, where the Manager, Bob Christie, has built up a schools league consisting of sixteen rinks from six schools, the youngsters play for a trophy donated by George Crabbie, for two years President of the Edinburgh Ice Rink Curling Club. Similar stories come from Ice Rinks up and down the country. In the new South of Scotland Ice Rink at Lockerbie, pupils from the Academy crowd on the ice in such numbers that a group of the youngest beginners play half-way up one rink, the other half of the same rink being used by a second group of new boys!

In the 1966–67 season, the National Schools Competition – carefully named so that schoolgirls, who have also started in Scotland, would not be precluded from the event – was introduced by the Royal Club. The trophy, purchased in Canada, was presented by John Monteith, a Grand Old Man of Scottish curling. Appropriately, four Hutcheson's boys, skipped by Campbell Dick, were the first winners, and, in 1968 and 1969, a Watson's rink skipped by Colin Baxter, won the event.

We can say with some certainty that the growth of Scottish schoolboy play came roughly twenty years after the High School boom in Canada. When news of the training schemes for Scottish youth reached Canada in 1962, Burd McNiece, Chairman of the Canadian School Curling Committee, wrote a letter of encouragement: 'This activity will expand rapidly. You are starting as we did nearly twenty years ago, since when School Curling has expanded beyond our fondest hopes until we have had for the past twelve years a Canadian Competition between rinks from each Province in round-robin play. It is estimated, now, that the competitions at School, Primary, Provincial and Canadian levels attract approximately 60,000 boys of High School ages.'

The first inter-provincial schoolboy competition in Canada was held in 1947 between boys from Manitoba, Saskatchewan and Alberta. In 1948, British Columbia and Quebec joined, and, in 1949, eight Provinces were represented. The first National Schoolboy Championship was held in Quebec City in 1950.

One interesting aspect of boy and girl curling in Canada which does not apply in Scotland is that remarkable phenomenon, the Jam Tin bonspiel. This is played by youngsters with jam tins filled with cement and with a rough handle attached on quarter-size outdoor rinks. Jam tin curling, which the young competitors play with as much earnestness and enthusiasm as their elder brothers in major competitions, is firmly rooted in Saskatchewan but played in many parts of Canada.

A new generation of curlers is springing up in Scotland. It is a wonderful opportunity for experienced curlers to pass on their experience and to put back something into the game they love. They can do this by teaching the traditional customs and courtesies and by stimulating the interest and enthusiasm of the young curlers with practice sessions, film shows, quiz evenings, and, if possible, the biggest thrill of all to a youngster – an away-from-home match against total strangers who will soon become friends.

CHAPTER TWENTY-FIVE

CURLERS' COURTS AND BEEF AND GREENS

NEW CURLERS BEWARE! Initiation at a Curlers' Court awaits you. You must be 'made' a curler. 'My Lord' will be in the chair, and, at his bidding, 'My Lord's Officer' will fence the Court for your benefit. You will be instructed in 'the mysteries' and you must listen carefully. There will be fun and frolic, and fines for doing wrong, and, sometimes, for doing right! The proceeds are auctioned at the end of the evening and are often given to charity.

You will be given the 'word' and shown the 'grip'. But we will say no more about this ancient ceremony – except to advise you to bring small change to pay the fines and not to put on your best suit!

> In canty cracks, and sangs, and jokes,
> The night drives on wi' daffin',
> And mony a kittle shot is ta'en
> While we're the toddy quaffin'.
>> From *Cauld, Cauld, Frosty Weather* by
>> the Rev. James Muir of Beith.

At Curlers' Courts and many curling suppers, the principal dish is 'Beef and Greens', the true curlers' fare. This excerpt from a Minute of the old Edinburgh Club in 1840 gives a fair indication of the eating habits of our ancestors: 'The bill of fare consisted of boiled salt beef and greens, haggises, sheeps' heads and broth, cockie-leekie and roast beef. The charge was 4s. 6d. each, including small beer and a bottle of whisky to each two members to be made into toddy.'

Another bill of fare, supplied to the members of the Noodle Club in Ayrshire in 1823, is even more formidable: 'hare soup, fried whitings, a large turbot, a joint of corned beef, roasted beef, corned pork, two tongues, chickens, a fine goose, four grouse, and vegetables, dumplings, pudding, custard, jam and jellies. A moderate proportion of wine was given and ale, porter and a modicum of drams.'

Our stomachs are less demanding in these straightened times! At a Beef and Greens supper, modern curlers are more likely to be offered Scotch Broth, Boiled Beef and Cabbage or Haggis and Neeps, followed by Biscuits and Cheese and Coffee.

But the spirit, and spirits, will be the same!

CHAPTER TWENTY-SIX

THE SCOTCH WHISKY CUP AND AIR CANADA SILVER BROOM

IN 1959, The Scotch Whisky Association presented the Scotch Cup, which was competed for by the champion rinks of Scotland and Canada. In 1961, the United States champions joined the event which was enlarged to include the Swedish champions in 1962. In 1964, when Switzerland and Norway entered the lists, the competition was played in Canada for the first time, in Calgary, where Alex Torrance and his young Scots rink failed in a gallant extra-end bid in the final. France made the event, now called the Scotch Whisky Cup, a seven-nations contest in 1966 and Germany joined the international gathering the following year to bring the competition to its present strength.

From its inception, James Woodhouse, Secretary of The Scotch Whisky Association, and the late Jock Waugh, Scotch Cup Director – a much-travelled curler who was known and admired in many curling countries – gave dedicated service to the world event and they will always be associated with the Scotch Cup, which, in nine years, grew from a competition between two countries to a World Championship between the top rinks in eight nations.

When The Scotch Whisky Association decided to discontinue sponsorship of the competition in 1967, the Royal Club negotiated for a replacement sponsor, and, on 15th January, 1968, the Royal Club and Air Canada announced that the Air Canada Silver Broom would replace the Scotch Whisky Cup. The debt owed by the curling world to The Scotch Whisky Association for creating the World Championship was stressed by Air Canada when they assumed sponsorship.

Apart from Calgary (1964), Vancouver (1966) and Pointe

Claire, Quebec (1968), the world event was held in Scotland since it was launched in 1959. Now, the 'Silver Broom', directed in 1968–1969 by Jack Bowen of Air Canada, will be staged, annually in March, in different curling areas of the world and the 1970 Competition will be played at Utica in New York State.

Canada has dominated the World Championship, the Canadian Winners from 1959 to 1969 being Ernie Richardson (1959, 1960, 1962, 1963), Hec Gervais (1961), Lyall Dagg (1964) and Ron Northcott (1966, 1968, 1969). Bud Somerville, U.S.A., broke the Canadian stranglehold on the event, in 1965, and Chuck Hay, long a contender in the competition, won the last Scotch Cup for Scotland, amid scenes of great excitement, on his home ice in Perth in 1967.

CHAPTER TWENTY-SEVEN

INTERNATIONAL CURLING FEDERATION

AN ATTEMPT TO form an International Curling Federation – a prerequisite for an application for curling to be included in the Winter Olympic Games – was made in June, 1957, when a Meeting was held in Edinburgh.

In 1965, because of the tremendous growth of the game in the world, the Royal Club again initiated plans for international Meetings, and, during the World Championship for the Scotch Whisky Cup in March 1965, invited office-bearers from overseas Associations to 'A Meeting of Administrators and Personalities' in Perth. At this Meeting, the President of the Royal Club, Major Allan Cameron of Allangrange, proposed that an International Committee of the Royal Club be formed. The Meeting agreed that the new body should be called the International Curling Federation and that a draft Constitution should be prepared.

Representatives of seven nations met during the Scotch Whisky Cup Competition in Vancouver in March, 1966, and it was agreed that, subject to the approval of at least three member countries, the Federation would be deemed to be established as from 1st April, 1966.

When the representatives met in Perth in 1967, the establishment of the Federation was confirmed and an amended Constitution was ratified. Rules for International Competitions, prepared by a sub-committee, were considered, and, at the following meeting, held in Pointe Claire, Quebec, in March 1968, these Rules were approved and adopted for the World Championship for the Air Canada Silver Broom.

Member countries of the Federation are Canada, U.S.A.,

Sweden, Switzerland, Norway, France and Germany, and these countries, with the Royal Club representation, form a Federation of eight nations. The President for the first two years was Major Allan Cameron and the Secretary is Robin Welsh. The Federation headquarters are the office headquarters of the Royal Club. Meetings of the Federation are held annually during the week of the World Championship, wherever the event is held.

CHAPTER TWENTY-EIGHT

POETRY, LITERATURE AND THE CLERGY

IT IS GENERALLY accepted that the earliest reference to curling is contained in *The Muses Threnodie, or Mirthfull Mourning on the Death of Master Gall,* by Henry Adamson (1638). An edition, with notes by James Cant, was published in Perth in 1774 and the poem, set in Perth, contains many interesting references to the Fair City. Adamson, George Ruthven, a doctor and surgeon, and James Gall were close friends, and, when Gall died young of consumption – despite the efforts of Ruthven, who collected and administered herbs from the hillsides at Kinnoull and Moredun – Adamson wrote an *In Memoriam* in which the following lines appear :

> 'His cougs, his dishes, and his caps,
> A Totum, and some bairnes taps;
> A gadareilie, and a whisle,
> A trumpe and Abercorne mussell,
> His hats, his hoods, his bels, his bones,
> His allay bowles, and curling-stones,
> The sacred games to celebrat
> Which to the Gods are consecrat.'*

In the same year, 1638, Robert Baillie, Minister at Kilwinning, wrote : 'Orkney's process came before us; he was a curler on the Sabbath day.' (The 'Orkney' mentioned, George Grahame, Bishop of Orkney, was deposed by the General Assembly on 11th December, 1638.)

The poem is generally known as 'Gall's Gabions', the word gabion meaning a collection of odd items or bric-a-brac.

Any reference to curling poetry, or curling literature in general, makes the reader immediately aware of the debt owed by the curling community to Ministers of the Church.

> Frae Maidenkirk to John o' Groats
> Nae curlers like the clergy.
> *Old Proverb.*

Ministers not only played the game, with skill and enthusiasm, but also wrote about it, composed poetry about it and added vitality to it with penetrating and humorous remarks on the ice and from the pulpit. A typical story tells of the Minister who dismissed his congregation with the words : 'My brethren, there's nae mair harm in saying it than in thinking it; if the frost hauds, I'll be on the ice the morn's morning at nine o'clock.*

Many curling clubs elect chaplains and the Chaplains of the Royal Club now serve for five-year periods. The Rev. A. Gordon Mitchell, a prolific curling writer and poet, was Royal Club Chaplain from 1920 until 1939. The present holder of the office, the Rev. Bob Daly, of the Rossie Club, Perthshire, is a keen and skilful curler and a man whose good companionship and wit make him a welcome guest at all curling functions.

The celebrated William Guthrie of Fenwick, Ayrshire, author of the *Christian's Great Interest,* was ordained at Fenwick in 1644 and eventually driven from his Kirk in the persecutions of the Covenanters in 1665, just before his death. But, in those twenty-one years, he left an indelible mark on the parish. His loofie stone (1645), which is still preserved in Craufurdland Castle, was well-known on the ice in Ayrshire, and, says his biographer, 'he used the innocent recreations which then pre-vailed – fishing, fowling and playing on the ice – which, at the same time, contributed to preserve vigorous health'.

Dr Alex Pennecuik (1652–1722) also praised the health-giving properties of curling. The doctor, the 'Laird of Romanno', published his prescription in 1715 :

---

* The Rev. John Kerr estimated that, of the 20,000 Scottish members of the Royal Club in 1890, 500, or one in forty, were clergyman.

> To Curle on the Ice does greatly please,
> Being a Manly Scotish Exercise;
> It Clears the Brains, stirrs up the Native Heat
> And gives a gallant Appetite for Meat.

Allan Ramsay (1685–1758) followed the same theme in his poem, *Health,* dedicated in 1724 to the Earl of Stair, four lines of which cover three sporting activities:

> Then on the links, or in the estler* walls,
> He drives the gowff or strikes the tennis-balls,
> From ice with pleasure he can brush the snow
> And run rejoicing with his curling throw.

Ramsay's best-known curling verse occurs in his Epistle to *Robert Yarde of Devonshire*:

> Frae northern mountains clad with snaw,
> Where whistling winds incessant blaw,
> In time now when the curling stane
> Slides murmuring o'er the icy plain.

James Hogg, the Ettrick Shepherd (1772–1835), famous poet and fiddler, was also a keen curler who was President of the Ettrick Club and a member of the Duddingston and Peebles Clubs. His poem, *The Channel Stane,* begins:

> Of a' the games that e'er I saw,
> Man, callant, laddie, birkie, wean,
> The dearest, far aboon them a',
> Was aye the witching channel-stane.

Chorus.

* Hewn stone – a reference to the enclosure of a real tennis court.

Oh! for the channel-stane!
The fell good game the channel-stane!
There's no a game that e'er I saw
Can match auld Scotland's channel-stane.

The Ettrick Shepherd's poem *Curling,* is also well-known. One verse testifies to the democratic nature of the game:

Here peer and peasant friendly meet,
Auld etiquette has lost her seat,
The social broom has swept her neat
Beyond the pale o' Curling.

Sir Walter Scott (1771–1832) used curling as a backcloth for one of his descriptive passages in *Guy Mannering*: 'On the frozen bosom of the lake itself were a multitude of moving figures – some flitting along with the velocity of swallows, some sweeping in the most graceful circles, and others deeply interested in a less active pastime – crowding round the spot where the inhabitants of two rival parishes contended for the prize at curling: an honour of no small importance, if we were to judge from the anxiety expressed both by the players and bystanders.'

The most famous of all verses on curling were written by Scotland's national poet, Robert Burns. Extolling the virtues of his friend, Tam, as a curler, Burns wrote, in his *Elegy on Tam Samson* (1786):

When winter muffles up his cloak,
And binds the mire like a rock;
When to the loughs the curlers flock
    Wi' gleesome speed,
Wha will they station at the cock?
    Tam Samson's dead!

> He was the king o' a' the core,
> To guard, or draw, or wick a bore,
> Or up the rink like Jehu roar
>   In time o' need;
> But now he lags on Death's 'hog-score'
>   Tam Samson's dead!

(The 'cock' is an old Scots word for 'tee'.)

In *The Vision* (1786), Burns also referred to curling:

> The sun had clos'd the winter day,
> The curlers quat their roarin's play.

The literature of the game in full of poetry – some good, some interesting and some plain doggerel. We will add three often-quoted verses from last century:

> When biting Boreas, keen and snell,
>   Wi' icy breath and a' that,
> Lays on the lochs his magic spell,
>   And stills the streams and a' that.
> For a' that and a' that,
>   Cauld winter's snaw, and a' that;
> Around the tee, wi' mirth and glee,
>   The curlers meet for a' that.

From 'Curling Song', by Henry Shanks, Bathgate, the blind poet.

> Aye may we play with social glee,
> Devoid of strife and snarling,
> Sae put it round, wi' three times three,
> To freedom, love, and Curling.

From 'White Winter on Ilk Hill', by
      Rob. Hetrick, Dalmellington.

Now fill ae bumper – fill but ane,
And drink wi' social glee, man,
May curlers on life's slippery rink
Frae cruel rubs be free, man;
Or should a treacherous bias lead
Their erring steps a-jee, man,
Some friendly inring may they meet
To guide them to the tee, man.

From 'The Music of the Year is Hushed', by the
Rev. Dr Henry Duncan of Ruthwell.

The first book on curling, *An Account of the Game of Curling*, was written by the Rev. John Ramsay (1811), and Ministers of the Scots kirk also contributed the two other major books published last century – *Curling, The Ancient Scottish Game*, by the Rev. James Taylor (1884) and *History of Curling* by the Rev. John Kerr (1890) – Kerr's scholarly book remaining the best work available* on the history and growth of the game.

Curlers still write poetry on their favourite game, although to a much lesser extent than in the more leisured hours in past centuries, and we must give extracts from two modern poems, both of which are full of the native humour which is an integral part of curling. The first, written by Albert Mackie, a poet of high repute in Scotland and a non-curler, commemorated the first victory scored by England for many years in the annual Scotland *v*. England international match – and could be called an elegy!

Ach, sound the pibroch in lament!
They're laughing frae Carlisle to Kent;
The Sassenachs the taunt are hurling,
They've beaten Scotsmen at the curling.

* The diminishing number of curlers who own a copy of the book do not let it out of their sight. The book is now very rare, and, if a copy finds its way to a bookshop – after the disposal of an estate, for example – it is quickly resold.

Auld Scotia greets, as efter Flodden,
The biggest setback since Culloden,
That England has achieved sic fame
At Caledonia's native game.

The second was written by John Hamilton, a keen Ayrshire curler whom we reckon to be the best Scots curler-poet of his time. The extract is the first verse from his *Winning of the Alton Cup* :

But let us no' forget our freen';
James Gibb, the skip, was unco keen,
But sic a hash ye never seen
Tae draw a shot;
He stood and gaped and blinked his een
Like some auld goat!

A year or two after the winning of the Alton Cup, we played against John Hamilton and James Gibb in an inter-city match at Ayr and recited the verse to James. He sat back in his chair, roared with laughter and called for a round of drinks! A delightful companion, he is also a much better drawer of a shot than John Hamilton gives him credit for!

As curlers often ask for the Curler's Grace, to use at their annual suppers, we add it now, with a shorter alternative, to end this chapter, while realising that Grace should have been said at the beginning!

O Lord, whase luv surrounds us a'
And brings us a' thegither,
Wha writes your laws upon oor herts
And bids us help each ither;
We thank Thee for thy bounties great,
For meat and hame and gear,
And thank Thee too for sna' and ice
Although we ask for mair;

Gie us a hert to dae what's richt,
Like Curlers true and keen,
To be guid freens alang life's road
And soop oor slide aye clean.

Or this alternative :

O Power abune whose bounty free
Our needs and wants suffices,
We render thanks for Barley Bree
And mate that appetises.

Be Thou our Skip throughout life's game
An' syne we're sure to win,
Tho' slow the shot and wide the aim
We'll soop each ither in.

CHAPTER TWENTY-NINE

KEEN, KEEN CURLERS

ENTHUSIASTS IN ALL branches of sport are described as 'keen'. There are keen golfers, keen shinty players, keen anglers. But only curlers are 'keen, keen'. The two adjectives have a special significance.

'I promise to be a keen, keen, curler' is the vow taken by all who are 'made' curlers at Initiation Ceremonies. What do the words mean?

They can be explained in three short sentences: 1. A curler is not a true curler if he is not a keen, keen curler; 2. A curler should play the game to the utmost of his ability; 3. A lackadaisical approach is anathema to the game.

To enlarge on the theme, we sometimes hear the claim: 'I don't mind whether I win or lose, the game's the thing.' The words do not ring true and the man who uses them would not be welcome on our side, or, for that matter, on the side against us.

A game of curling should be played at one tempo – flat out – and with one aim – to win. Teams imbued with the will to win are rewarded with the most enjoyable and exciting play. This does not mean that curlers should be tensed-up and inhibited with thoughts of victory; that they should mount hate campaigns against their opponents and play with tight lips and without humour. Quite the opposite. A sense of humour is part and parcel of the game and the best sportsmen are those who respect sport sufficiently to want to play the game the best way they know how.

The Rev. A. Gordon Mitchell, a dedicated Chaplain to the Royal Club, preached a Curlers' Sermon in Woodside Parish

Church, Glasgow, in 1937. He used as his text: Chronicles',
chapter 12, verse 2 – 'Hurling Stones' – and delivered a stone
which deserves to be remembered:

'Not to be keen to win is an injustice not only to the curler's
own side but also to the side that opposes him. The true curler
never queers his pitch, never pulls his course, but strains every
nerve to win, and thus, whether he wins or loses, preserves his
own self-respect and the respect of his own rink and that of
the rink playing against him. Not to be in earnest in the game
is not to play curling but only to play *at* curling. If that is
the spirit in which anyone plays, I would remind him that,
although it may not matter very much whether we win or lose,
it does matter very much whether we play the game, and we
cannot play the game without being loyal to our side; in other
words, without doing our utmost to come out on the winning
side.' The mental approach to curling is a study in itself. At
the competitive level, a desire to win separates the players at
the very top from the players very near the top. The urge for
victory, the exercise of mind over matter, undoubtedly works,
in the same way as a golfer can 'will' a crucial putt into the
hole.

It follows naturally, and is perfectly consistent with a positive
will-to-win attitude, that curlers must be good losers. To lose
gracefully is essential in curling, as in all games, and, if that
virtue is not inbred in a curler, he must develop it. Undoubtedly,
the best way to achieve this is to play more and more games
because, as a popular Skip remarked, when congratulated on
accepting defeat with a smile: 'Oh, I'm a good loser all right;
I've had plenty of practice!'

In addition, a player has a much better chance of being a
good loser if he has fought every inch of the way and given all
he knows to win. He could not have done more.

Take your defeat like a man! Nothing looks worse on the
ice than a losing curler who throws down his broom in disgust.
It is *he* who is disgusting. Fortunately, very few let themselves
and the game down in this way. The handshakes all round,
which end every game of curling in every curling country in

the world, are followed by a friendly drink, laughter and perhaps a song later. The social glass tastes even better after a hard, keenly-fought and sporting game.

Dr John Renton of Penicuik, proposing the toast, 'A' Keen Curlers,' at the Grand Caledonian Curling Club Dinner in 1843, said: 'On Keenness the great value of curling depends. It is the principle of action, and intercourse too, and forms the great charm of attachment, not only to the game but which brings and binds curlers together. This attachment I neither can nor is it necessary for me to describe. It must be felt and it is not confined to the time we are engaged in the game nor to the season we enjoy it in; it lasts all the year through and dies only with the curler himself.'

The Doctor was referring to the *spirit* of curling, that elusive force which cannot be captured and enjoyed unless the curler gives himself completely to the game. The moral is clear: be a draw player or striker, stone-breaker or candlestick-maker, but, for goodness sake, be keen. And, in the words of the old Duddingston battle cry, 'Strain ilka nerve, shouther, backbane and hough'* to win. Then, win or lose, enjoy yourself. *That* is the spirit of curling!

* From a song, composed by Sir Alexander Boswell and sung by him at a Duddingston Society dinner in 1817.

CHAPTER THIRTY

THE FELLOWSHIP OF THE GAME

For on the water's face are met,
Wi' mony a merry joke, man,
The tenant and his jolly laird,
*The pastor and his flock, man.**

THE FELLOWSHIP OF curling is the hallmark of the game. The tradition was established in the far reaches of the first Clubs. Old Minute Books are full of charitable intentions and decisions to help the needy sections of the community, the earliest acts of curling fellowship being the playing of matches for bolls of meal for the poor.

The first Regulation of the Duddingston Society was: 'Resolved that the sole object of this institution is the enjoyment of the game of curling, which, while it adds vigour to the body, contributes to vivacity of mind and the promotion of the social and *generous* feelings.'

Penalties and fines were imposed on curlers for a long list of offences, from swearing on the ice to introducing a political topic. Some of the money collected was diverted to the needy but most of the gifts were the result of challenges between parishes and clubs. Charitable funds were created and food and eldin (fuel) were distributed to widows, orphans and the poor. Benevolence was a feature of old-time curling.

Politics has always been a forbidden subject in curling. Among the Rules of the Ardoch Club in Upper Strathearn, instituted in 1750, was: 'No politics of Church or State to be discussed.' Many other Clubs followed this example in their printed Rules.

* From *The Music of the Year is Hushed,* by the Rev. Henry Duncan, D.D., of Ruthwell.

Dr Norman McLeod's curling song, first published in *Blackwood's Magazine,* underlines the point:

It's an unco' like story, that baith Whig and Tory
Maun aye collyshangy, like dogs owre a bane;
An' that a' denominations are wantin' in patience
For nae Kirk will thole to let ithers alane.
But in fine frosty weather, let a' meet thegither,
Wi' brooms in their hauns an' a stane near the 'T';
Then, ha! ha! by my certes ye'll see hoo a' pairties
Like brithers will love and like brithers agree.

The democratic nature of the game is aptly summed up by a famous parody on Burns:

Ours is a game for duke or lord,
Lairds, tenants, hinds, an a' that;
Our pastors too, wha preach the Word,
Whiles ply the broom for a' that.
For a' that and a' that,
Our different ranks an' a' that,
The chiel that soops and plays the best
Is greatest man for a' that.
                    Old Song.

The easy and natural intermingling of all classes on the ice led to chapters of happy accidents, volumes of humour. The stonemason was directing the Sheriff who had more than once sent him to prison for poaching. 'Noo, Shirra,' shouted the skip, 'dae ye see that stane?' 'Aye, Jock', answered the Sheriff. 'A weel, just gie that ane sixty days!'

At the Jubilee Dinner of the Royal Club in 1888, Lord Balfour told of a conversation on the train to a Grand Match at Carsebreck. A curler looked up from his morning newspaper and said: 'I see, Geordie, that you are drawn against a lord to-day.' Geordie thought for a moment before answering quietly: 'Maybe I'll be the lord before night!'

The Earl of Eglinton was directed by a famous curler, Hugh Conn, to strike out a stone. Watching the Earl's stone with

anxious excitement, the redoubtable Hugh was heard to shout:
'Bravo, my Lord; Bravo my Lord; Bravo, —— oh Lord, I
declare ye wad miss a haystack!'

We cannot stress too strongly, for the benefit of beginners who
do not yet know and older curlers who may have forgotten,
that curling is fun and that any curler who does not enjoy
himself is missing the whole point of the game. When once asked
on Television, 'And why do you curl?' our impromptu answer
was 'To have fun'. On reflection, we would not change it.

The banter and wit among curlers has created a literature of
its own, which is nurtured and enlarged by overseas tours. The
fun and *faux-pas* of a tour are remembered for a lifetime.
When the 1957 Scottish Team returned from Canada, we invited six of the tourists to reminisce and placed a tape-recorder
behind a sofa. The tape, 45 minutes of gentle chaffing, hilarious
story-telling and conclusive evidence of international friendship,
remains a treasured record of the real stuff of curling tours.

> True feelings waken in their hearts,
> An' thrill frae heart to hand,
> O! peerless game that feeds the flame
> O' fellowship in man!
> The Rev. T. Rain.

What more can we say about the camaraderie of Curling?
New curlers, who listen to speeches at dinners and presentations, will hear a great deal about it – and it is all true. We
state this categorically and in the certain knowledge that it is the
most important statement in this book: fellowship is the highest
point, the greatest virtue in Curling. The life blood of the game,
it flows through every company of curlers, from the four members of a rink to the large congregation on a loch or at
an annual meeting; and the lasting friendships formed on overseas tours, which increase in number each year, bring ever
nearer to fulfilment the principal aim of the Royal Club –
'to unite Curlers throughout the world into one Brotherhood
of the Rink'.

INDEX

Note: page numbers in italic indicate illustration

179